A Short Introduction
to Hermeneutics

A Short Introduction to Hermeneutics

David Jasper

Westminster John Knox Press
LOUISVILLE • LONDON

Book design by Sharon Adams
Cover design by Mark Abrams

First edition

Published by Westminster John Knox Press
Louisville, Kentucky

This book is printed on acid-free paper that meets the American National Standards Institute Z39.48 standard. ♾

Printed in the United States of America

04 05 06 07 08 09 10 11 12 13— 10 9 8 7 6 5 4 3 2 1

Library of Congress Cataloging-in-Publication Data

Jasper, David.
    A short introduction to hermeneutics / David Jasper.
        p. cm.
    Includes bibliographical references and index.
    ISBN 0-664-22751-1 (alk. paper)
    1. Bible—Hermeneutics.   I. Title.

BS476.J37 2004
220.6'01—dc22   2004043018

For David Klemm
Friend, Colleague, and Interpreter
par excellence

Contents

Preface

This short introduction to hermeneutics has grown directly out of years of classroom teaching, mainly in the University of Glasgow and most recently in the University of Iowa. In the last two years, the Department of Theology and Religious Studies at Glasgow has developed a distance-taught degree in religious studies, and this proved to be a golden opportunity to set my increasingly dog-eared lecture notes out into a more comprehensible, ordered, and up-to-date form. That is the immediate basis for this book.

It is, therefore, very modest in its aims and objectives (to use the ghastly "quality assurance" parlance of the modern university). Its scholarship is, I trust, well founded, but it makes absolutely no claims to originality. Indeed, quite the opposite, for my aim is to give the reader a good grounding in the basic issues and in historical information on which further thought and reading may be built. It is limited very largely to the Western Christian tradition and its roots in the interpretation of the Bible.

Generations of students have contributed ideas, and I thank all of them! My colleagues in Glasgow, Marije Althorf, Darlene Bird, Andrew Hass (now of the University of Stirling), and Sarah Nicholson, have helped me teach this material at one time or another, and especial thanks go to them. Dr. Nicholson, in particular, was the genius behind the distance-taught degree, and has labored valiantly over lecture notes to make them comprehensible and coherent outside the walls of the traditional classroom.

For most recent help, I must thank Professor David E. Klemm and his colleagues in the Department of Religious Studies at the University of Iowa. The bestowal on me of an Ida Cordelia Beam Visiting Professorship in the spring semester of 2003 gave me the space and time actually to write the book and put it into its present expanded form.

The German nineteenth-century theologian and scholar Friedrich Schleiermacher reminds us that the task of hermeneutics is never finished. Reading is an art as much as writing, and a skill with many parts. This book is just a first step along the road, but one that will, I hope, set the reader in the right direction with a little more confidence and mindful of the company of many who have gone before and acquired a little wisdom in their travels.

The New Revised Standard Version of the Bible is used throughout.

Introduction

Donald K. McKim begins the Introduction to his book *A Guide to Contemporary Hermeneutics* (1986) with a fine understatement that is nevertheless profoundly true! "To launch into the field of hermeneutics is a major undertaking." The student of the present book will encounter issues in a bewildering range of intellectual disciplines, frequently, it seems, at odds with one another: historical inquiry, literary studies, philosophy, theology, and more. This small work is intended only as a brief introduction to this hermeneutical minefield, but I hope a useful one, inasmuch as it seeks to provide the reader who has little or no prior knowledge of the subject with a map that will enable him or her to get around a little more easily as the going becomes tougher later on. Its background is largely limited to the Western Christian tradition and its ways of reading the Bible, as a way to more general questions about texts and reading and the issues facing us in our contemporary cultural situations. It makes no claims to be more than a beginning, but it will, I trust, provide a good foundation for the future. As important as any information that it contains are the questions it poses. It must be made clear from the start, however, that to these there are no final or correct answers.

"Hermeneutics" is not a word we use in everyday English, but it is a useful technical term to describe our understanding of the nature of texts and how we interpret and use them, especially with respect to the Bible, a collection of ancient texts with distinctive

1

and abiding authority. How we read and understand the Bible has constantly changed across the millennia of its history in both the Jewish and Christian traditions. Indeed, the problem of hermeneutics begins actually *in* the Bible itself, as we shall see, and part of this book will be a sort of Bible study. It will look at the way in which it is impossible to read the Bible without acknowledging that processes of interpretation are going on even in the canon of Scripture. It is pretty clear, for example, that the author of Matthew's Gospel is reading and interpreting the Gospel of Mark and adapting it for his own theological purposes, and that all four Gospels are different "interpretations" of the life and passion of Jesus. In the Hebrew Bible (that is the term I prefer to use for what is also broadly known as the Old Testament, which implies the Christian interpretation of an originally Jewish collection of documents), books are continually interpreting and reinterpreting one another.

For instance, 1 and 2 Chronicles are essentially a rewriting of the books of Kings to suit a different culture, and different theological and even different ethical requirements. We need to be aware of what is happening in such a process. Part of this process is also the history of the development of the *canon* of Scripture, to which some attention will be given. Understanding a book is not simply a matter of looking at how it was *written*, but also the history of how it has been *read* and accepted as authoritative.

The aim of this book is to give students an understanding of the importance of hermeneutical reflection for religious thought and understanding in the broad context of the Bible and later Christian theology, noting the historical and philosophical contexts of the subject as it develops from the earliest days of the Christian church to the present day. It offers a general introduction to the history of Christian hermeneutical inquiry, and it will also provide a theoretical basis for beginning to understand the processes of hermeneutics in different faith traditions, such as Judaism and Islam. These are only very briefly alluded to, and the reader should not expect anything like comprehensive descriptions of the huge range of hermeneutical possibilities that lie outside the limited parameters of this small book. But we shall see, for example, how at least an awareness of them can indicate that the Christian and Western understanding of such terms as "text," "reading," and "meaning" is actually quite limited and by no means should be taken as universal or absolute. When the contemporary French hermeneutical thinker Paul Ricoeur asked in a very difficult essay (anthologized in David Klemm's two-volume reader *Hermeneutical Inquiry*), "What Is a Text?" he was indicating that this is by no means the simple question we might assume it to be and that, as we shall see, the rabbinic tradition has an answer to it very different from a tradition that derives essentially from Greek philosophical ways of thinking and understanding.

Indeed, hermeneutics is about the most fundamental ways in which we perceive the world, think, and understand. It has a philosophical root in what we call *epistemology*—that is, the problem of how we come to know anything at all, and actually how we think and legitimate the claims we make to know the truth.

My hope is that after working through this book, the reader should be in a position to understand and reflect on the history and theory of interpretation in the West, both in the context of biblical study and in the range of disciplines taught in departments of religion and seminaries. I hope that it will also be useful for all students of literature, whether they are concerned with the Bible or not. Its purpose is to provide a point of reference for students and teachers from which they can advance to further thought and study. From it the reader will be able to acquire a clear knowledge of biblical hermeneutics from a historical perspective as well as an introductory knowledge of the theoretical and philosophical issues that underlie their development. In addition, this knowledge will be closely related to contemporary questions in literature, religion, and theology and the place and authority of the Bible in our culture.

This book therefore serves a very different function from that of a standard work like Robert Grant's *A Short History of the Interpretation of the Bible*, being at once more limited and at the same time more comprehensive. Behind Grant's work lies a vast library of biblical and historical/theological scholarship. My concern is much more interdisciplinary and rooted in my fundamental interest in the relationship between literature and religion, which is about how texts function, about the processes of reading, and about how these questions impact immediately on religious and theological questions. It is thus, in the end, as much about reading novels and poems as it is about reading the Bible.

Because this is a study book, and indeed grows directly out of my own classroom teaching, at the end of each chapter there are questions and suggested topics for discussion and reflection. These are, of course, only suggestions, and can be safely ignored if you wish. Some of them are in the form of group exercises and some are simply essay questions that have proved useful to students over the years. From time to time I have also introduced some practical examples of hermeneutics for the reader within the texts of the chapters. For instance, at the end of chapter 2 (pp. 42–43) there is a passage from Augustine's *City of God* that raises a number of issues in interpretation, but it is left up to the reader to work at these himself or herself. In other words, my hope for this book is not simply that you will *know* more about hermeneutics, but that you will become a better reader yourself—and this latter aim is by the far the more important.

Recommended Reading

There are a number of useful readers in hermeneutics. They provide brief excerpts from original texts with notes and explanatory commentaries, and are a helpful way into some of the primary material covered in this course.

(The books marked ** are strongly recommended, and those marked * are recommended.)

**Klemm, David E., ed. *Hermeneutical Inquiry.* Two vols. AAR Studies in Religion 43/44. Vol. 1, *The Interpretation of Texts*; Vol. 2, *The Interpretation of Existence.* Scholars Press, 1986. (This is the best overall introduction to the subject.)

Mueller-Vollmer, Kurt, ed. *The Hermeneutics Reader.* Blackwell, 1985. (This deals only with the eighteenth century to the present day. It is not specifically concerned with religious questions, but is an excellent introduction to the primary critical issues.)

The Best Introductions to the Subject

**Jeanrond, Werner G. *Theological Hermeneutics: Development and Significance.* Macmillan, 1991. (Recently republished by SCM Press. Clear, straightforward, and essential reading. This deals with both ideas and the historical development of the subject as a category of theological thinking.)

*McKim, Donald K., ed. *A Guide to Contemporary Hermeneutics: Major Trends in Biblical Interpretation.* Reprint Wipf & Stock, 1999. (A very useful collection of essays indicating the range and complexity of the subject, by major authors.)

*Thiselton, Anthony C. *New Horizons in Hermeneutics: The Theory and Practice of Transforming Biblical Reading.* HarperCollins, 1992. (Large and unwieldy, but a comprehensive mine of information.)

Other Useful Texts

Barton, John. *The People of the Book? The Authority of the Bible in Christianity.* SPCK, 1988.

Bleicher, Josef. *Contemporary Hermeneutics: Hermeneutics as Method, Philosophy and Critique.* Routledge and Kegan Paul, 1980.

Bruns, Gerald L. *Hermeneutics Ancient and Modern.* Yale University Press, 1992. (This is a series of essays that looks also at non-Christian hermeneutics, for example, the issues raised by the reading of the Qur'an.)

Caputo, John D. *Radical Hermeneutics: Repetition, Deconstruction, and the Hermeneutic Project.* Indiana University Press, 1987. (This is a difficult book, not for the fainthearted, but one of the best introductions to contemporary and postmodern hermeneutics.)

Gabel, John B., Charles B. Wheeler, and Anthony D. York. *The Bible as Literature: An Introduction.* 3d ed. Oxford University Press, 1996.

Grant, Robert M. with David Tracy. *A Short History of the Interpretation of the Bible.* 2d enlarged ed. Fortress Press, 1984. (A reliable, standard work.)

Jasper, David. *The New Testament and the Literary Imagination.* Macmillan, 1987. (A simple and straightforward introduction to New Testament interpretation, which covers particular questions concerning such matters as narrative, proverbial form, the problem of history, and the nature of biblical poetry.)

Jost, Walter and Michael J. Hyde, eds. *Rhetoric and Hermeneutics in Our Time.* Yale University Press, 1997.

Loades, Ann and Michael McLain, eds. *Hermeneutics, the Bible and Literary Criticism.* Macmillan, 1992.

*Lundin, Roger, Anthony C. Thiselton, and Clarence Walhout. *The Responsibility of Hermeneutics*. Eerdmans, 1985. (Recently reprinted. This is a clear and straightforward defense of why hermeneutics is important.)

Morgan, Robert with John Barton. *Biblical Interpretation*. Oxford Bible Series. Oxford University Press, 1988.

Prickett, Stephen and Robert Barnes. *The Bible*. Landmarks of World Literature. Cambridge University Press, 1991.

Ricoeur, Paul. *Figuring the Sacred: Religion, Narrative and Imagination*. Edited by Mark I. Wallace. Fortress Press, 1995. (A selection of essays by Ricoeur that provide a very good introduction to his work and thought.)

Schleiermacher, Friedrich. *Hermeneutics and Criticism, and Other Writings*. Edited by Andrew Bowie. Cambridge University Press, 1998. (The best and most accessible way into this pivotal figure in the history of hermeneutics through selections of his writings, with an excellent critical introduction that sets Schleiermacher in historical and philosophical context.)

Wadsworth, Michael, ed. *Ways of Reading the Bible*. Harvester Press, 1981. (This book, now sadly long out of print, is a series of fascinating essays on different issues in biblical hermeneutics through particular texts such as the parables of Jesus.)

Chapter One

Texts and Readers: Reading and Writing

1 Introduction

The word *hermeneutics* is an English form of the classical Greek word *hermeneus*, which means an interpreter or expounder—one who explains things. At one point in the writings of the philosopher Plato, poets are described as "interpreters of the gods." Throughout this book I will use the rather unusual term "hermeneut," rather than, say, "interpreter," in order to be true to this tradition. In Greek mythology Hermes was the messenger of the gods, noted for his speed and athleticism, whose job it was to carry to the people of earth the messages and secrets of the gods of Olympus. With his winged sandals Hermes was able to bridge the gap between the divine and human realms, putting into words those mysteries which were beyond the capacity of human utterance. Without such a messenger how would these two realms communicate with each other, and how would the gap in the understanding between the gods and humankind be overcome? His task was to bridge this gap and to make that which seems unintelligible into something meaningful and clear to the human ear.

Hermeneutics, then, is about "interpretation" or even "translation," and especially the interpretation of sacred texts, which believers may understand as in some sense divinely inspired or "the word of God." Much of this book will be about how people through the millennia have interpreted the Bible, the sacred Scriptures of both the Jewish and the Christian traditions, though references will occasionally be made to other sacred texts such as the Muslim Qur'an and the Hindu Bhagavad Gita. Nor is this unrelated to the wider questions of how we read anything at all, and how we understand or too often fail to understand the texts that we read; how we frequently disagree among ourselves about the meaning of texts, or how some texts that we find deeply meaningful can seemingly have no meaning at all for other readers. At the same time, reading is not just a question of seeking meanings. Texts can affect us in many ways. They can make us angry, or frightened, or they can console us. *Writing*, then, is a kind of action that can work on us in ways far beyond our mere understanding. This is sometimes called the "literature-as-action" model, which regards texts not simply as language but as performance and action. Texts can make us *do* things as well as *understand* meaning. One thing will, I hope, quickly become clear— hermeneutics is never static: how we read and understand the nature of a text is changing all the time, just as we ourselves change in our self-understanding. Indeed, what we actually mean by "reading," "text," and even "author" is very complex and actually not at all self-evident. And so we must start with a review of these apparently very simple terms so that as we begin to approach the history of Western hermeneutics we may be a little more wary and suspicious. We must begin by upsetting a few assumptions that we have perhaps made too readily, and acknowledge that maybe we understand a little less about first principles than we imagined.

2   Faith and Suspicion, Texts and Readers

At the beginning of the nineteenth century, the English romantic poet Samuel Taylor Coleridge maintained that as we read a text (he was actually referring specifically to poetry) it must be with "that willing suspension of disbelief for the moment, which constitutes poetic faith" (*Biographia Literaria*). To read anything requires, if you will, an initial act of faith in the text before us. In other words, if we are reading a novel, we have to believe that the hero is a real person, who matters to the reader even though we know that this is "just fiction." The text becomes a "world" which we inhabit for a while ("for the moment"), participating in its drama and its claims on us. We can find instances of how this textual world can affect a whole public. In Victorian England, for example, so great was the public outcry at the first ending of Charles Dickens's novel *Great Expectations*, in which the lovers Pip and Estella are condemned to a life apart, that the author had to write another ending, which brought the lovers together so that Pip can finally say, "I saw no shadow of another parting from her." His reading public breathed again and felt much better. People's lives can be deeply influenced by a text, even though we know that it is just "made up," just an imaginary world. Such fictional texts and narratives can be pretty powerful in our lives, even though we *know* that, in a sense, they are not "true." We *believe* in them, and we are drawn into their worlds and the lives of the characters who inhabit those worlds. How much more has this been so of sacred Scripture! That collection of texts which Christians call their Bible (a title derived via French and Latin from the Greek word *biblia*, which just means "books," or a collection of scrolls stored in a chest or cupboard) has been immensely powerful in the history of Western culture, engendering tremendous faith and belief, arguments and even wars, and thereby effecting enormous outcomes in people's and nations' lives, for both good and ill.

Perhaps we may come to the Bible and read it with the eyes of faith, believing every word (or most of them), and believing that it is "a pantry of wholesome food, against mouldy traditions; [and] . . . a fountain of most pure water springing up into everlasting life" (words from "The Translators to the Reader" prefixed to the Authorized Version of the Bible of 1611). This response we call a "hermeneutics of faith." As we shall see, a hermeneutics of faith can take many forms, but it was, on the whole, the predominant way of reading the Bible for at least the first fifteen hundred years of Christian history.

On the other hand, we may come to read a text with caution, even skepticism, determined to test every claim and proposition against such humanly defined standards as the light of reason or the evidence of history. This we call a "hermeneutics of suspicion," and it has characterized most (though not all) thinking about hermeneutics in the past three or four hundred years. As we shall see in this book, these two attitudes of faith and suspicion are actually present in almost all acts of reading and interpretation in one way or another, sometimes more the one, sometimes more the other.

On the whole, it must be said, we do have a tendency to believe what is written down in a text, even though no less an authority than Plato, in his dialogue called *The Phaedrus*, warns us against the claims of the written word and the difficulty of interpreting it. After all, we cannot interrogate the text or ask it to explain itself more clearly as we can a speaker, whom we can ask to pause and repeat what has just been said in a different way or define for us an unfamiliar word that we have heard. To such demands the text can only remain silent. Thus Socrates warns his friend Phaedrus:

> Once a thing is committed to writing it circulates equally among those who understand the subject and those who have no business with it; a writing cannot distinguish between suitable and unsuitable readers.

And so he concludes:

> And [the] writer, past or future, who claims that clear and permanently valid truth is to be found in a written speech, lays himself open to reproach. (Plato, *The Phaedrus*, trans. Walter Hamilton.)

Ironically, of course, the same thing can be said of Plato's text itself!

And yet, still, the written word has considerable authority, and above all we seek there for *meaning*. Almost invariably the first question asked by a pupil given a difficult book to read is, "What does it *mean*?" This would seem to presuppose a clear, objective meaning or content to be "excavated" from the text, provided we have the right tools and are clever enough to do it. Yet actually what we mean by "meaning" is not altogether clear if you stop and think about it.

Second, we often try to make a clear distinction between texts that deal in facts and therefore claim to be "literally" true, and texts that are fictional or "made up." Actually the distinction between the literal and the literary truth is extremely difficult to pin down. "Literally" basically means "according to the letter," and in biblical interpretation relates to a grammatical and *non-metaphorical* understanding of the "letter" of Scripture. Its relationship to the "truth," however, is extremely difficult to define, and the literal is often closely associated with the historical. Thus, many Christians, especially in the nineteenth century, discouraged the reading of novels and works of fiction because they were "not true," while the Bible, as the Word of God, was regarded as both true and historically accurate. As we shall see, however, the sense in which, say, the Gospels are "true" or "historical" is fiercely debated throughout the history of hermeneutics. We sometimes speak of the "literal truth" as if a "literal reading" (whatever that means) stands in sturdy contrast to the vain imaginings of metaphor or other rather vaguely understood terms. Metaphors (the word is derived from two Greek words, *meta phero*, which mean to "carry over") are suggestive of displaced meaning. Something does not *really* mean what it appears to say, and so we cannot speak *literally* of the kingdom of heaven; we can only describe it metaphorically as being "like" something more familiar. In Mark's Gospel Jesus asks, "With what can we compare the kingdom of God, or what parable will we use for it?" (Mark 4:30). The word "parable" is very like metaphor, derived from the Greek, and meaning that which is "thrown alongside" or parallel to the literal truth. In fact, the idea that a text, least of all a biblical text, may have just one *meaning*, which, once grasped, remains firm, absolute, and unchanging forever, is a relatively modern concept, and an odd one at that, and would have been very alien to an early Christian interpreter, or

> The word "parable" is very like metaphor, derived from the Greek, and meaning that which is "thrown alongside" or parallel to the literal truth.

hermeneuts like Origen of Alexandria (ca. 185–254), Augustine of Hippo (354–430), or even Thomas Aquinas (1225–74), all of whom we shall turn to in later chapters.

One of the effects of reading, apart from acquiring information (and part of the task of hermeneutics is to establish criteria to enable us to begin to distinguish between true and false information), is to stimulate us into thought and action. "Using our imaginations" actually may be a very good and creative thing, and retarding the imagination, especially in children, a negative or even dangerous policy. Texts that require the exercise of the imagination may provoke us into ethical reflection or aesthetic appreciation, although there is certainly a *wrong* use of the imagination as well. But the imagination may properly carry us beyond the limitations of systems of thought or even the orthodoxies of religion.

The English writer Edmund Gosse, in his book *Father and Son* (1907), wrote an account of his Victorian childhood under the tutelage of his evangelical parents, who feared the imagination and believed in the literal truth of the Bible and the terrible dangers of "fiction."

> Never in all my early childhood [wrote Gosse], did anyone address to me the affecting preamble, "Once upon a time!" I was told about missionaries, but never about pirates; I was familiar with humming-birds, but I had never heard of fairies. Jack the Giant-killer, Rumpelstiltskin and Robin Hood were not of my acquaintance, and though I understood about wolves, Little Red Riding Hood was a stranger even by name. So far as my "dedication" was concerned, *I can but think that my parents were in error thus to exclude the imaginary from my outlook upon facts.* They desired to make me truthful; the tendency was to make me positive and skeptical. (Gosse, *Father and Son*; emphasis added)

What do you think Gosse is saying here? Why should the exclusion of fairy stories and the exercise of the imagination from childhood tend to make one skeptical? Are there any stories in the

Bible like the ones he refers to? (I did warn you that this is a book that does not provide all the answers!)

Texts, you see, can offer to us more than literal, historical, or scientific truth. Actually, such categories that we tend to take for granted are often relatively recent in the history of human understanding. The writer of Matthew's Gospel, for example, as we shall see later, would have had no concept of what we now mean by the word "history" or its claims in our systems of inquiry. And so, if words like "literal," or "meaning," or even "text" itself are beginning to become a little more difficult and problematic for you, then we are actually getting somewhere, for it is the business of hermeneutics to get us to think rather more carefully than we are wont to do about just such words, and so perhaps to be a little less absolute in our claims to understand them. Hermeneutics warns us also about taking too simply and straightforwardly the idea that a text is just exactly what it was intended to be in the mind and intention of its author, as if understanding the letters of Paul were equivalent to entering into the mind and purposes of the apostle himself. Too often people will say "Paul" when they actually mean the text of the "Letter to the Romans." The careful reading of the letter should avoid the over-simple equation of Paul and his text, and we sometimes call this too straightforward conflation the *intentional fallacy*—that is, the fallacious belief that Paul's intentions in writing are utterly and without reserve reflected in the text of his letter. Why this is a fallacy can be simply illustrated, for now, by the familiar words "I never quite say what I mean, and I never quite mean what I say." When you are writing an essay or paper, is it always the case that you are able to find exactly the right words to encapsulate what (you think) is in your mind? Do we not often struggle to express our thoughts, often remaining dissatisfied that we have done so adequately in our writing? Or, is it not the case that someone may read your essay and remark, "Do you realize what you have said and its implications?" To which you can only humbly reply, "No, I did not mean to say this and I will try and do better next time." No more are Paul's great letters entirely and simply a statement of his conscious intentions. Texts, we might say, have a life of their own, and as Plato warned us, they are always in danger of being misinterpreted, for no one is a perfect reader or a perfectly controlled writer.

You will find an excellent verbal exercise on this point in Lewis Carroll's *Alice in Wonderland*, when Alice becomes confused at the Mad Hatter's tea party:

> "Then you should say what you mean," the March Hare went on. "I do," Alice hastily replied; "at least—at least I mean what I say—that's the same thing, you know." "Not the same thing a bit!" said the Hatter. "Why you might just as well say that 'I see what I eat' is the same thing as 'I eat what I see!'"

Hermeneutics recognizes this slippage between intention and meaning, or worse, between the slipperiness of written words and human understanding. One and the same text may be understood very differently by different people—one will be persuaded of the "truth" of the book of Revelation, another will find it tedious nonsense. It is important to realize that neither is necessarily right or wrong, but we must establish some rules for judgment. We need also to bear in mind that our understanding of a text is not simply dependent on universal principles that are equally shared by all, but depends on such things as age, gender, cultural assumptions, and so on. Also, as readers we change—I do not understand things the same way now that I am in my fifties as I did when I was in my twenties. These are obvious points, but they need to be kept clearly in mind. In hermeneutics we must think for ourselves, but at the same time we cannot just make up the rules as we go along, regardless of other people, tradition, or, indeed, the conventional claims of language and its grammatical rules. We cannot be content to be like Lewis Carroll's Humpty Dumpty when he says, rather inconsequentially, to Alice, "There's glory for you!"

> "I don't know what you mean by 'glory,'" Alice said. Humpty Dumpty smiled contemptuously. "Of course you don't—till I tell you. I meant 'there's a nice knock-down argument for you!'"

"But 'glory' doesn't mean 'a nice knock-down argument,'"
Alice objected.

"*When I use a word*," Humpty Dumpty said in a rather
scornful tone, "*it means just what I choose it to mean—neither
more nor less.*" [Emphases added.]

"The question is," said Alice, "whether you *can* make
words mean so many different things."

"The question is," said Humpty Dumpty, "which is to be
master—that's all."

(Lewis Carroll, *Through the Looking Glass*; emphases added)

Now, of course, we cannot, like Humpty Dumpty, simply
choose what words mean. We cannot finally be their master,
choosing meanings at will. The result would be a total breakdown
in all agreement about meaningful communication, and we would
respond to all language, whether written or spoken, with Alice's
"I don't know what you mean." End of story. We reach the point
of what Humpty Dumpty calls "impenetrability"—which is when
he gives up on the subject altogether. But words are not finally
impenetrable. When I shout "Help!" I want to be pretty certain
that you understand what I mean. When the road sign says "Stop,"
we know what to do—and we know the probable consequences of
not so acting! And by general consensus we *do* understand enough
in common to be able to say, "I can [that is, I am able to] read the
Gospel of Mark," though perhaps only in a translation from the
original Greek. (*Translation* is another issue taken up by
hermeneutics.) We can read the words and get a pretty good idea
of what is going on. Certainly we inevitably reflect in our reading
our differences and our prejudices, although the fact that some of
us do not necessarily believe that the first verse of the Gospel is
actually true does not prevent us from reading the book *as though
it were true*, and getting a great deal out of the exercise. Above all,
we need to recognize that although we can read the *words* (perhaps with the help of a dictionary), we have very little idea what it
was like to *be* a first-century Christian in the Roman Empire.
Mark's Gospel is a text that is culturally far removed from us in its
origins, and we must be careful, as readers, not simply to impose

our own modern presuppositions and prejudices on it. This gap between cultures has been called "the two horizons" (by the modern hermeneut Hans-Georg Gadamer, whom we shall be looking at later on): that is, the "horizon" of the origins of the text, almost two thousand years ago, and the "horizon" of the contemporary reader who seeks to make sense of it in the modern world.

We are all different. If you give one text to thirty people, you will come up with more or less thirty different "readings," none of them, perhaps, wholly wrong or wholly right. True, there will be a great deal of overlap, and when a powerful institution like a church seeks to impose uniformity on our reading (in the interests of orthodoxy or order), we can be persuaded pretty well all to think alike. But the fact remains that what is called "reader-response" to a text is various and often contradictory, especially with authoritative, often patriarchal, texts like the Bible. Two people may read the same words, and one will laugh while the other will weep, and they will not understand each other. Such differences make it all the more important that we attend to the discipline of hermeneutics that tries to maintain legitimacy, order, and discipline in the midst of these many claims. It may also teach us to learn to live creatively with our differences from one another.

3   Reading and Writing

One of the first things most of us learn very early as a child is the art of reading and writing. As literate people we tend to take these skills for granted, though we should never forget that literacy is the privilege of the relatively few in human history. Yet we need to pause and reflect that not only do these terms refer to very complex activities, but also that people's understandings of them, and of the nature of a text, are not fixed and static but have changed through the course of history and will continue to change. There are many different answers to the question "What is a text?"

How we understand what a text is, is also deeply affected by technology—the development from the scroll to the codex (or book) affected how people wrote and read. The availability of words to us in different media makes a great difference in how we understand words. The invention of the printing press was profoundly influential on Martin Luther's biblical hermeneutics, for reasons which we shall see later on, while the effect of computers and the World Wide Web on reading and writing can hardly yet even be contemplated. (It is, however, commonplace for people to say that their style of writing is changed in the shift from pen and paper to keyboard. Indeed, some of us rarely "write" at all these days, but punch keys and watch the effect on a screen.)

> It is commonplace for people to say that their style of writing is changed in the shift from pen and paper to keyboard. Indeed, some of us rarely "write" at all these days, but punch keys and watch the effect on a screen.

Actually the change from the handwritten to the printed word, as we shall see in more detail when we come to consider the work of Martin Luther, altered the whole way in which the world was perceived and understood, shifting communication from dependency on the vagaries of the individually copied text (with all its inevitable "mistakes"), to texts that guaranteed uniformity and could be endlessly reprinted on the production-line model. Marshall McLuhan has shown us the startling consequences of this change.

> The uniformity and repeatability of print permeated the Renaissance with the idea of time and space as continuous measurable quantities. The immediate effect of this idea was to desacralize the world of nature and the world of power alike. The new technique of control of physical processes by segmentation and fragmentation separated God and Nature as much as Man and Nature, or man and man. (McLuhan, *Understanding Media: The Extensions of Man*)

We shall see later how hermeneutics in the nineteenth and twentieth centuries have been preoccupied with recovering a sense of *wholeness* in the business of interpreting texts, overcoming the disintegration of our thinking into different, discrete disciplines.

It is from the Greek tradition and works like Aristotle's *Poetics* (ca. 350 B.C.E.) that we gain our assumptions that texts "have meaning" and characteristically have a clear beginning, middle, and end with a unity that brings about a conclusion, after which nothing more can really happen. "They all lived happily ever after" means that this is the end of the story, and there is nothing further worth telling. For a concise statement of this you might refer to Aristotle's *Poetics*, chapters 7 and 8. (This is easily available as a Penguin Classic.) The Christian tradition, which was strongly influenced by Greek thought, has interpreted the Bible against this background, seeing it as a unified and complete "book" with a clear beginning, middle, and end. The scholar M. H. Abrams, in a classic study of Romantic literature of the eighteenth and nineteenth centuries, sees the Christian way of reading the Bible, from the earliest times, as characterized in a number of particular ways:

1. "Biblical history is finite. It represents events as occurring once and once for all, in a single closed temporal span." The Bible is essentially a historical document, and in the main the events that it describes from beginning to end actually happened to real people like you and me. Thus it is that scholars of the Bible, at least during the last two hundred years, have largely followed the methods of "historical criticism."

2. "The design of biblical history constitutes a sharply defined plot with a beginning, a middle, and an end, and a strongly accented sequence of critical events." In other words, the Bible has the structure familiar to most stories or novels.

3. "The plot of history has a hidden author who is also its director and the guarantor of things to come." Unlike novels, however, whose authors we immediately identify as Jane Austen, Charles Dickens, or Mark Twain, the Bible has been regarded as "written" in some sense by God. And so at the end of Bible readings in church we will frequently conclude with the words, "This is the word of the Lord." (See Abrams, *Natural Supernaturalism*)

Now, we have to be clear that none of these things about the Bible are *necessarily* true. They are the consequence of a particular way of reading and understanding how texts work. In short, they are the consequence of a specific hermeneutical strategy, which is at once the *result of* a theological perspective and also *results in* a theological perspective in a kind of circular or *dialectical* movement. A certain belief dictates how we read the Bible, and reading the Bible in this way confirms that this belief is true or at least legitimate. (This is an example of the *hermeneutic circle*, which will be explained in more detail a little later on. Furthermore, it is essential to realize that there are many other "ways of reading" and of understanding the "written" nature of the biblical texts than this primarily historical model.)

In the next chapter we will compare this very briefly with quite different and more ancient traditions of reading and textual understanding of Scripture, both Jewish and Christian, though before we do we need to recognize, by way of comparison, that distinct again are the hermeneutics of the Muslim Qur'an and the Bhagavad Gita of Hinduism. Although they will not concern us much further here, it is well to have some sense of other sacred texts.

Unlike the Bible (which has always from the beginning been a translated text—there have been over three hundred and fifty translations into English alone) the Qur'an properly cannot be translated. Gerald Bruns describes this succinctly in his book *Hermeneutics Ancient and Modern*:

> It is not enough to speak of the Qur'an as a text. Rather, it is the recitation (*qur'an*) of a text that only God has seen, the *umm al-kitab*, literally, "Mother of the Book." . . . As a text the Qur'an exists only within quotation marks. The Qur'an cannot be fixed as a text, even though the texts . . . are fixed and remarkably consistent with one another. The hermeneutical consequences of this fundamental orality are many and complex. For example, the translation of the Qur'an is not so much forbidden as it is materially or, say, ontologically impossible. . . .

. . . as a recitation the Qur'an surrounds us with itself, fills the space we inhabit, takes it over and ourselves in the bargain. The whole movement of reading as an appropriation or internalizing of a text is reversed. Here there is no grasping and unpacking and laying the text bare. On the contrary, reading is participation. To understand the Qur'an is to disappear into it. (Bruns, *Hermeneutics Ancient and Modern*)

The Bhagavad Gita comprises eighteen chapters of the great Indian epic poem the *Mahabharata*. Written in the context of the war to be fought by Arjuna, it is frequently claimed that the value of the poem lies in its reconciliation of many and varying views within Hinduism and the freedom it grants to different understandings and interpretations. Thus Mahatma Gandhi, who read the Gita in its entirety every week, replied serenely to the question as to whether the poem teaches both *himsa* (violence) and *ahimsa* (nonviolence):

> I do not read that meaning in the Gita. It is quite likely that the author did not write it to inculcate ahimsa, but as a commentator draws innumerable interpretations from a poetic text, even so I interpret the Gita to mean that if its central theme is anasakti [selfless action], it also teaches ahimsa. (Quoted in Gwilym Beckerlegge, ed., *The World Religions Reader*)

Clearly Gandhi is not concerned with *the* meaning of the text, and certainly not the intentions of its author as a guide to interpretation!

4   The Hermeneutic Circle

We referred above to the *hermeneutic circle*, and in the next chapter we shall review it also in the context of an early Christian theologian, Irenaeus, bishop of Lyons (ca. 130–ca. 200), and his principle of *regula veritatis* or "canon of truth." But before we go any farther it will be wise to give some attention to this immensely important issue in hermeneutics, for it is essential that we understand it clearly. Look at it in this way.

The Bible is the origin and primary source of Christian doctrine and the belief of the church. At the same time, this very belief, known as the *apostolic tradition*, is the "canon of truth," which regulates our proper reading of Scripture. In other words, Scripture provides the rule by which the interpretation of Scripture is tested. (Martin Luther, indeed, believed that the Bible was its own interpreter.) But which comes first—text or interpretation? The answer is neither and both. The German theologian and philosopher Friedrich Schleiermacher (1768–1834), often known as the father of modern hermeneutics, and whom we shall consider in more detail in chapter 4, described this circularity of the hermeneutic process in this way: In order to gain an overview of the text in its completeness, we must give proper attention to the details and particulars. But we cannot appreciate the significance of these details and particulars without a sense of the whole work. We begin with the big idea, read the text clearly and in detail in the light of this, and then use the text to substantiate the initial idea.

Interpretation, therefore, is not a process along a linear trajectory from ignorance to understanding via the medium of the text. By the end of this first chapter, I hope you will have some sense that it is far more complicated and actually more interesting than that. The reading process, in its various forms, does not provide us with any final conclusion (except, perhaps, when we finally come to rest at the end of all things in God) but an endless stimulation to further inquiry and conversation. And as the German philosopher Martin Heidegger (1889–1976) once remarked, what is important is not how we get *out* of the hermeneutic circle (which, arguably, is impossible anyway), but how we initially get *in*. In other words, what idea do you start with—one based on faith or one based on suspicion, or, more likely, a mixture of the two? What are your presuppositions, your presumptions, and your prejudices? These may not necessarily be either good or bad—but we all have them! All of them will have a bearing on how you read and interpret.

The purpose of this first chapter has been to raise questions and, hopefully, disturb a few assumptions. By now you may be feeling a little perplexed and even a little disgruntled! People often complain that the study of hermeneutics only makes things more difficult, when they actually should be quite simple and straightforward. Well, as we now continue with a brief history of hermeneutics in the Christian West, with its discussions about the nature of texts (especially, though not exclusively, the Bible) and how we read, we shall see that it has never been either simple or straightforward. Indeed, hermeneutics is inseparable from the development of Christian theology and doctrine, and has often been highly contested and political. In some ways the whole of the Reformation emerges from and centers on the hermeneutic revolution provoked by Martin Luther, John Calvin, and their fellow reformers.

The end of the book, I must warn you now, will leave us with further questions, which are prompted by our particular cultural situation at the beginning of a new century. We live as perhaps never before in a multicultural society deeply influenced by faiths and traditions other than Christian and Jewish, and for many by a profound rejection of *all* faith traditions. It was partly for this reason that this chapter has included very brief introductions to the sacred texts of Islam and Hinduism. But at the same time we live, some would say, in a "postmodern" (or even "post-postmodern") age of skepticism and relativism in which nothing is stable and no beliefs accepted as final; an age profoundly affected by the revolutions of such modern "prophets" as Sigmund Freud (in psychology) and Albert Einstein (in science), not to speak of Karl Marx (in politics) or Friedrich Nietzsche (in philosophy). All these thinkers, like them or not, have had their effect on the way we read and understand texts, and not least the "sacred" texts of Scripture.

We have a long way to travel yet, but at least we have started. We need now to proceed with a healthy mixture of faith and suspicion, and a readiness to think hard!

Summary

We might summarize the main points of this chapter as follows:

1. Hermeneutics is understood as interpretation, the word drawn from the name of the Greek god Hermes, who is the "messenger of the gods."
2. Hermeneutics is a mixture of a hermeneutics of faith and a hermeneutics of suspicion. What do we mean by "text," and what do we mean by "reading"?
3. Aristotle and the Greeks understood a text as a unified whole with beginning, middle, and end. The modern reading of the Bible has been largely in the light of this understanding of the nature of text, but this need not necessarily be the case.
4. We have encountered the problem of the hermeneutic circle and the "never-ending story" of interpretation.
5. Great religious traditions, apart from the Jewish and Christian, have their own distinctive hermeneutics and "ways of reading" their sacred texts.

Activities and Questions

1. Some texts inspire faith, while others arouse our suspicion. How do we get the balance right? Are there objective criteria to help us achieve this balance?
2. Imagine that you are reading a book and encounter a word that you have never seen or heard before, and you have no idea what it means. The dictionary gives you three different meanings, and it is not clear at first sight which is most appropriate. How would you set about deciding on a proper and defensible understanding of the word in this context?
3. Writing of poetry in his *Poetics*, the Greek philosopher Aristotle remarked that "a likely impossibility is always preferable to an unconvincing possibility." What do you think he meant by this? Think of this particularly in relation to the passion narratives of the Gospels. (Don't worry if this leaves

you puzzled—in hermeneutics it is often more important that you think hard and carefully than that you reach the "right" answer.)

4. For this activity you will need other members of your family or colleagues. Read carefully two biblical passages, preferably in a modern English version.

   Genesis 22:1–14
   John 1:1–18

   Don't worry so much about what these passages *mean* (whatever that means!), but try to assess how they affect you, and therefore *how* you read.

   For example, will a woman read the Genesis passage differently from a man?

   To what extent are you reading with a hermeneutics of faith or a hermeneutics of suspicion? You may well find that people vary enormously in this. (Refer back to your answer to question 1, above.)

   How does this make a difference to your manner of reading? Do you feel angry, perplexed, consoled, or what?

   Then compare notes with others—be prepared to argue if necessary! (Hermeneutics has always been about arguing and debating much more than agreeing on the correct answer. No reading is wholly right or wholly wrong. We may just have to learn to live with our differences.)

5. What do you think Martin Heidegger meant when he said that it was more important to consider how we *enter* the hermeneutic circle than any possible way out? Does this mean, perhaps, that good reading is more about being aware of ourselves and our predispositions than about "getting the right answer"? What do you think?

Chapter Two

Midrash, the Bible, and the Early Church

1 Midrash and Rabbinic Interpretation

Before we briefly review the emergence and development of early Christian hermeneutics, it is important to be aware of the even more ancient traditions of Jewish interpretation, and we shall concentrate on the term *midrash*, while remembering that this is merely a glance at what is an immensely rich and complex tradition that blends into later Christian understanding and has undergone something of a renaissance in recent literary and biblical studies. Midrash represents only one aspect of ancient Jewish exegetical methods, though an extremely important one. (For further guidance you might look at Werner Jeanrond's book *Theological Hermeneutics*, pp. 14–17.)

The Jewish scholar Jacob Neusner defines midrash quite simply as "biblical exegesis by ancient Jewish authorities." The word derives from the Hebrew *darash*, which means to "study," "investigate," or "search." (*What Is Midrash?* p. xi.) Neusner goes on to break the term down into various categories, but my purpose here is both simpler and more specific and briefer. It is generally to indicate that the ancient Rabbis had a very different understanding of text and reading from that which we have been broadly considering so far.

If the Greek tradition is essentially philosophical, the Hebrew tradition is not. The Jews did not so much seek meaning *in* words, but rather saw in words a form of conversation, which is endless and reaches no conclusion, unless it is finally enclosed in the silence of God with which everything begins and ends. There is no closure to text, but endless repetition and refinement—not even necessary agreement among interpreters, but discussion in the "space" provided by writing. And so the very concept of *text* itself must be revised.

The Torah, that is, the divine order of life as written in the five books of the Law, or Pentateuch, which also constitute the first books of the Christian *Old Testament* from Genesis to Deuteronomy (to be distinguished from the Jewish *Hebrew Bible*), in the rabbinic view is not actually an artifact of nature. In a sense it was not ultimately even written by human agency, but was in being even before the creation itself. Here is a famous midrash (or commentary) on the first verses of the book of Genesis:

> It is customary that when a human being builds a palace, he does not build it according to his own wisdom, but according to the wisdom of a craftsman. And the craftsman does not build according to his own wisdom; rather he has plans and records in order to know how to make rooms and corridors. The Holy One, blessed be He, did the same. He looked into the Torah and created the world. ("Midrash on Genesis," quoted in Susan Handelman, *The Slayers of Moses*)

For the ancient Rabbis, then, the text of the Torah is the blueprint of all creation, existing in a sense before all else. Now, the actual written, physical letters that we read are to be seen as the "garments of Torah," the clothing of the preexistent "text," so that even the very form and shape of the marks in the page have profound significance and meaning. This is the basis for the verse in that most Jewish of Gospels, Matthew, when, during the Sermon on the Mount, Jesus says that "until heaven and earth pass away, not one letter, not one stroke of a letter, will pass from the law until all is accomplished" (Matt. 5:18). The older English version that refers to the "jot and tittle" of the law is actually referring to the small Greek letter *iota* (jot), and even a single pen stroke ("tittle" or "title" in earlier English). Even the strokes of the letters of the Torah are eternal. Thus reading and interpretation of Torah is not just an exercise in trying to understand its meaning, with the text merely a kind of means to that end of understanding. It is much more than that, for the material text of the Torah is nothing less than the enclothing of the nonmaterial original, divine Torah, which is infinite and infinitely mysterious. We might say that just reading the words of Torah is a physical act rather like touching the hem of the garment of the divine.

So, against this background the process of interpretation, or midrash, is necessarily also endless and a sort of process toward the finally unutterable divine. There is never a moment when you can stop and say conclusively, "Now I understand this," for this is not the purpose of reading, and even to presume to make this claim would constitute a misunderstanding. It would be to claim to understand what is beyond our understanding. One modern Jewish interpreter, the literary critic Geoffrey H. Hartman, has described reading as a "struggle for the text" (or even, the struggle with the text). Just as wrestling Jacob struggles with the mysterious stranger in Genesis 32:22–32, so the reader encounters the mystery of the Torah, demanding, like Jacob, to know the mystery of "the name," or identity. It is worth reading that passage again as a model of reading. Jacob, having crossed the Jabbok, wrestles alone all night with the unknown opponent, as you might struggle into the dark hours with the text before you. He is even wounded in the fight, but he persists and seeks to wrest the mystery out of the stranger, saying, "I will not let you go, unless you bless me." What we seek from the text is not meaning so much as a blessing on us, and we should be prepared to struggle with it even if wounded by its mystery, until we achieve this. We seek to know the mysterious "name" of the text.

But what is important is not any conclusion that we may reach, but rather the struggle itself, and what Hartman calls its "frictionality." Reading can generate heat from our encounter with its narratives, and reading can send us away from the book like Jacob from the stranger, damaged in the fight, so that we may limp from our encounter with the text—perplexed and wondering, yet also wiser. And if we do not finally understand in any intellectual sense and remain puzzled by what we read, we might do well to recall the words of one commentator on the Genesis text, that as we struggle with texts, "it is no sin to limp." Reading may, in a sense, wound us, but that may be a positive thing, even though painful.

2   Hermeneutics in the Hebrew Bible and the New Testament

The distinction that we make between a "primary" text and the "secondary" processes of criticism is a relatively recent one. Of recent date also is our idea of the "ownership" of a text and its ideas by its author, protected under strict copyright laws. The authors of the Hebrew Bible, whoever they were, borrowed freely from earlier literatures of the ancient Near East, shaping and adapting texts for their own theological purposes, and the older strata of a text sometimes remain close to the surface, like hard ancient rocks that resist the weathering of time and remain visible in a landscape of a later geological date.

For example, read Genesis 6:1–4, the description of the people of the earth before the Flood.

> When people began to multiply on the face of the ground, and daughters were born to them, the sons of God saw that they were fair; and they took wives for themselves of all that they chose. Then the LORD said, "My spirit shall not abide in mortals forever, for they are flesh; their days shall be one hundred and twenty years." The Nephilim were on the earth in those days—and also afterward—when the sons of God went in to the daughters of humans, who bore children to them. These were the heroes that were of old, warriors of renown.

Who are these mysterious "sons of God" who have children by the daughters of humans, and the Nephilim ("strong ones," or "heroes") who "were on the earth in those days"? Their roots are probably in ancient Mesopotamian origin stories.

Or again, it is more than likely that the book of Job is based on a much more ancient epic poem, adapted for later use. Indeed, a great deal of the Hebrew Bible is almost like a running commentary on texts from earlier cultures of the ancient Near East. Furthermore, narratives in the Hebrew Bible are repeated and told again with different emphases suited to different theological or cultural purposes. Biblical critics have long argued for different strands of authorship in the Pentateuch, the first five books of the Hebrew Bible (traditionally thought to have been the compositions of Moses himself), sometimes called the JEDP narratives (Yahwist, Elohist, Deuteronomic, Priestly). This textual layering would account for the two versions of the creation story that appear in the first three chapters of Genesis, each with its own specific concerns and understanding of the story. Clearly these ancient authors were shaping traditional material with their own hermeneutical principles of interpretation, driven by distinctive theological visions. (Theology and hermeneutics, as we shall see time and again in the pages to come, are never far apart.) Later on we have two accounts of the Ten Commandments in Exodus and Deuteronomy. On a larger scale, as we have already briefly noted, the two books of Chronicles begin with a rapid genealogy from Adam, and then pick up the history of the Davidic kingdom, which was also recounted in the four books of Samuel and Kings, but with careful editing to suit their own purposes. For example, the shady episode of David's encounter with Bathsheba and his disposal of her husband, Uriah the Hittite, is carefully elided. David's character has to be reinterpreted.

Throughout the Hebrew Bible there are examples of readings and editing of earlier texts, fragments of which remain within the canon of Scripture, reminding us that hermeneutics has always been a religious and political activity and that no reading is "innocent" of motives that seek, in the popular phrase, to accentuate the positive and eliminate the negative.

As we move on to the New Testament (the formation of whose canon or shape we shall consider in a little while), we find that not only are great parts of it in the form of commentaries or readings of the Hebrew Bible, but it was not long before the Christian church interpreted and edited the Hebrew Bible for its own purpose, making of it the Christian Old Testament. (That is why it is important to keep these two terms Hebrew Bible and Old Testament separate and distinct, even though they are largely comprised of the same material.)

One example of such revisionary reading of the Hebrew Bible is in the Sermon on the Mount in Matthew 5–7. Here Jesus takes the Ten Commandments and offers a new, ethical account of them. "You have heard that it was said to those of ancient times. . . . But I say to you . . ." (5:21–22). He insists that his purpose is not to change or dispense with the ancient text. Ancient Jewish exegetes regarded every word of Scripture as spoken by God, and Jesus is not dislodging this principle. What he is doing is offering a new interpretation of the Decalogue (the Ten Commandments) based on different hermeneutical principles that change not so much its *meaning* as its *significance* for us. Its effect, therefore, becomes rather different. Jesus says to his listeners that what they always thought they had understood is now to be taken in a new way. Our understanding of texts is never static.

Furthermore, Matthew, which is the most Jewish of the Gospels, begins (rather like 1 Chronicles) with a genealogy that links Jesus directly with Abraham, the father of the nation, and then recounts the story of the nativity precisely so that it is "according to Scripture." The author of this Gospel is not concerned with the questions of modern historical analysis or resolving for us the "quest for the historical Jesus" (to which we shall come in due course), and indeed, such things would have been quite incomprehensible to him, for our concept of history is a relatively recent invention. The evangelist's concern is to show that Jesus is the fulfillment of all the prophecies of the Hebrew Bible, and insofar as he is this, he is confirmed as the expected Messiah. Everything happens "according to Scripture." In short, the evangelist reads the Hebrew Bible in the light of later events, and he reads later events in the light of the Hebrew Bible—a perfectly good hermeneutic circle! (This is actually a principle taken up in the modern interpretive process in New Testament studies that is known as *redaction criticism*, although I suspect that sophisticated redaction critics

The hermeneutical circle is a principle taken up in the modern interpretive process in New Testament studies that is known as *redaction criticism*, although I suspect that sophisticated redaction critics would not like to admit it! But the principle is simple: you take the events of a narrative to establish a universal thesis, and you then use the universal thesis to interpret and confirm the truth of the narrative in all its details. Like all hermeneutics, it brings you round in a circle!

would not like to admit it! But the principle is simple: you take the events of a narrative to establish a universal thesis, and you then use the universal thesis to interpret and confirm the truth of the narrative in all its details. Like all hermeneutics, it brings you round in a circle!)

Another key to the reading of the Hebrew Bible in the New Testament is *typology*, and the principle of typological reading is to remain extremely important throughout the history of Christian hermeneutics at least until the Middle Ages, in both texts and the visual arts. Figures, and sometimes events in the Hebrew Bible, are seen as prefigurements of persons and events in the New Testament, and thus their authenticity is guaranteed by ancient prophecy or foreshadowings. For example, the birth of Jesus is seen in the light of the sign that is given in Isaiah 7:14:

> Therefore the Lord himself will give you a sign. Look, the young woman is with child and shall bear a son, and shall name him Immanuel.

(It is interesting to note, given its later importance in Christian theology, that the idea of *virgin* here is present only in the later Greek text of the Bible known as the Septuagint, and not in the original Hebrew. Can we say that later doctrine is the result of a textual accident—that the author of Matthew's Gospel was using the Greek and not the Hebrew text?) Typological readings of the Old Testament gathered importance in Christian biblical understanding. Isaac, for example, the son who was almost (though not quite) slaughtered by his father in Genesis 22, becomes a type of Christ (who does die as a sacrificial lamb in obedience to his Father's will—see Luke 22:42).

In the letters of Paul, the "type" in the Hebrew Bible becomes closer to an *example*, or at times an *allegory*. Either way, it is clear that Paul reads the Old Testament (we can call it that in his case) as being in perfect continuity with the events of Christ's passion and the New Covenant in him, a principle that was to be extremely important in the hermeneutics of the reformer Martin Luther. For example, we can read the whole narrative of the Exodus as a warning to Christians not to behave as the ancient Israelites did. "Now these things occurred as examples [types] for us, so that we might not desire evil as they did" (1 Cor. 10:6). Thus we can learn from reading of the example of those who lived under the old dispensation. Elsewhere, Paul reads the Old Testament as an allegory that illustrates and explains the new times in which we live in Christ. In Galatians 4:22–26, he takes Abraham's two sons, one born from Sarah, and the other, Ishmael, born of the slave girl Hagar, and proceeds to describe the two women as the two covenants:

> Now Hagar is Mount Sinai in Arabia and corresponds to the present Jerusalem, for she is in slavery with her children. But the other woman corresponds to the Jerusalem above; she is free, and she is our mother.

The first "is" of this statement is certainly not intended to imply any literal claim. Paul is simply using the text to illustrate and exemplify his point. It is a way of reading.

But above all we need to recognize how Paul is reading the Old Testament *christologically*. (Again it is easy to see why Luther was so drawn to the Pauline letters.) Christ is the second Adam, whose Passion reverses the Fall effected by the first Adam. Everything else follows from this, and this becomes the hermeneutical key by which the Old Testament is to be read, and by which the Hebrew Bible becomes Christianized as a sort of interpretive blanket that is spread over it, explaining everything in terms of its later fulfillment in Christ, in whom law is superseded by grace. Indeed, what Paul does is impose a theological vocabulary on his reading of the text that guarantees its meaning in the light of the redemptive work of Christ. (We might reflect whether we, in our own way, often impose a theological vocabulary on the texts of the Bible in order to make them "make sense." Do you think that this is the case?)

But before we leave the texts of the New Testament and enter into the hermeneutics of the early Christian church itself, a final word of warning is in order. Paul has in common with the author

> We might reflect whether we, in our own way, often impose a theological vocabulary on the texts of the Bible in order to make them "make sense." Do you think that this is the case?

of Matthew's Gospel a background in Jewish thought and an understanding of the Jewish Scriptures. This, however, is not necessarily true of all the literature of the New Testament, and we should not expect hermeneutical consistency from its canon. Here is an example of what I mean.

The Letter to the Hebrews (once thought to be by Paul, but pretty certainly not from his pen) draws a picture of Christian continuity with the Old Covenant between God and his ancient people, the Jews, who were not wrong, but merely incomplete without Christ, who is the "pioneer and *perfecter* of our faith" (emphasis added). The epistle looks back to the faith of Abraham and Moses and the whole great "cloud of witnesses" who people the pages of the Hebrew Bible, and who yet cannot "apart from us [as Christians], be made perfect." Thus it opens with the words:

> Long ago God spoke to our ancestors in many and various ways by the prophets, but in these last days he has spoken to us by a Son, whom he appointed heir of all things. (Heb. 1:1–2)

But now turn to the speech of Stephen to the Jewish council in Acts of the Apostles 7, and you will find a very different reading of the Hebrew Bible as a history of willful refusal to listen to the voice of God speaking through Moses and the prophets. And so Stephen accuses his Jewish opponents and their ancestors as murderers to the present day. It is easy to see here how this particular reading of Scripture could give rise to a profound anti-Semitism, just as later readings of the Bible (as we shall see) have given rise to such things as apartheid or, more broadly, the effective enslavement of women. You see how awareness of interpretive processes is not just an academic exercise. *How we read* a text can have the most profound effects on how we see other people and how we behave toward them.

Very shortly after the age of the apostles, Ignatius, bishop of Antioch, who was martyred in Rome ca. 110 C.E., affirmed confidently that the prophets of the Old Testament "lived in accordance with Jesus Christ" and for this reason they were in their time persecuted by the Jews. Ignatius clearly read the Old Testament as a Christian document.

3   The Establishment of the Christian Canon and the Argument from Tradition

For the first Christians the only Scripture was the Hebrew Bible. But there is some evidence that from the very beginning there was an impulse to establish authoritative texts from within Christianity itself. One theory suggests that as early as the end of the first century of the Christian era (C.E.), the writing of the book known as the Acts of the Apostles led to the earlier letters of Paul being collected, and they were certainly widely known, though not regarded at this stage as "scriptural." The first record of an attempt to establish a Christian "canon" of Scripture dates from the middle of the second century and is the work of the heretic Marcion, all of whose works were destroyed. Marcion would have excluded from the canon all of the Hebrew Bible and included only Luke's Gospel and a few of the Pauline letters. (The origin of the word "canon" lies in classical Greek, being understood as a straight rod or stick, used as a rule or standard—a "yardstick." The texts of the canon are thus those by which all others are measured and interpreted as orthodox or heretical. Literary tradition has continued to use the term *canon* to refer to texts that have become established as preeminent, such as Shakespeare, Dante, or Milton,

The origin of the word "canon" lies in classical Greek, being understood as a straight rod or stick, used as a rule or standard—a "yardstick." The texts of the canon are thus those by which all others are measured and interpreted as orthodox or heretical. Literary tradition has continued to use the term *canon* to refer to texts that have become established as preeminent, such as Shakespeare, Dante, or Milton, though this literary canon is far less well defined that than of the Bible.

though this literary canon is far less well defined that than of the Bible.)

Marcion's work was violently rejected, but it pointed up the urgent necessity of establishing clear and authoritative texts on which the Christian church could build its belief and theology. Perhaps the most important figure in this process of settling the "canon" of the New Testament is Irenaeus, bishop of Lyons from about 177 C.E. Irenaeus established the canonicity of the four Gospels (from a plethora of other so-called "apocryphal Gospels"), appealing rather bizarrely to unlikely Old Testament authorities like David and the fact that the cherubim on which the Lord's presence sits were four-faced! The point is that the confirmation of stable authoritative texts was a crucial factor in establishing Christian self-definition.

Irenaeus and his disciple Tertullian of Carthage (ca.160–ca.220) both wrote strongly against the hermeneutical principles of the gnostic Valentinus and his followers, and their criticism, for our purposes, can be summed up in two forms. (Gnostics, very broadly, believed in special knowledge gained either from the apostles or by direct revelation from God. Their teachings often involved strange and convoluted interpretations of Scripture.) First, Irenaeus accuses the Valentinians of picking and choosing the order of the scriptural passages, changing things around to fit in with their own ideas and heretical theology. By contrast, Irenaeus himself insists that we take Scripture as is, and we are not at liberty to change the order of the texts to suit ourselves. Second, they make complex and obscure what is actually clear and straightforward in their reading of Scripture. More interested in their own gnostic ideas than the texts themselves, the Valentinians simply make things more complicated than they actually are! Both Irenaeus and Tertullian insisted on interpretation based on tradition, a *regula veritatis* (canon of truth) that is the faith that is preserved in the church right back to the apostles themselves, true to the claim of the *apostolic succession*. In short, this was a hermeneutics based on *authority* and *continuity*, and to read Scripture was to situate oneself within the entire history and order of the church.

For Tertullian, who seems to have had legal training, the Scriptures belonged to the church, which inherited them from the apostles, and therefore it was impossible to read them outside its context. In his book *De praescriptione hereticorum*, which argues that the heretics outside the church are not to be allowed to read Scripture, Tertullian asserts:

> For there, where it will appear that the truth of Christian discipline and faith are found, there also will be the true scriptures, the true interpretations, and all true Christian traditions. (Quoted in Robert M. Grant, *A Short History of the Interpretation of the Bible*)

If the church alone is granted the right to interpret Scripture, we can see how this limits the possibility of any individual understanding of the text. Interpretation is to be in unity with all other right-minded and orthodox readers. Those outside the church must be, by definition, wrong! Try to think what defining contexts affect your own reading—such as religious belief, culture, political creed, etc.

> Try to think what defining contexts affect your own reading—such as religious belief, culture, political creed, etc.

4   The School of Alexandria and the School of Antioch

Nevertheless, early Christian thinkers inherited a fundamental problem from Jewish hermeneutics, that is, whether the interpretation of Scripture should be *literal* or *allegorical*. Quite quickly there were established two major schools of thought in the church, one based at Alexandria in Egypt, which inclined to an allegorical or symbolic reading of Scripture, and the other in Antioch, a much more Jewish city, which was more interested in reading Scripture literally.

Let us take Alexandria first. To begin with, we need to realize that this was a highly cosmopolitan and learned city, far removed from the Western world of Irenaeus and Tertullian. The earliest great scholar of the Alexandrian school, Clement (d. ca. 214), was broadly educated by teachers from all over the world of the eastern Mediterranean, both Greek and Jew, although at the same time, like Irenaeus, Clement insisted on interpretation that was in accord with the "true tradition of the blessed teaching straight from the holy apostles Peter and James, John and Paul" (Clement, quoted by Eusebius in his *Ecclesiastical History*). At the same time, Clement was influenced by the Jewish thinker and exegete Philo of Alexandria (ca. 13 B.C.E.–45 or 50 C.E.), who read the Hebrew Bible through the eyes of Greek philosophy and argued that frequently the literal sense of Scripture must be set aside in favor of the allegorical sense. Also, Philo regarded a text as having not one meaning, but many. Philo's thinking was eclectic, and ultimately he saw no difference in the truth to be found in Greek philosophy or the truth of the sacred text. He was also close to the kind of rabbinic reading that we looked at in the beginning of this chapter, where every letter of the divine text is significant and full of deep meanings.

Clement follows this hermeneutical lead in his understanding of Scripture as a language of symbols, to be understood allegorically, although his guiding principle (unlike Philo) was faith in *Christ the Word* or *Logos*, speaking in the Old Testament as in the New. Reading with this principle, Clement is content to follow at least five possible senses of the text of Scripture: the historical, the theological or doctrinal, the prophetic, the philosophical, and the mystical. Above all, Clement is concerned with theology and a theological vision for which the Bible provides a kind of map or a resource on which he draws freely to construct his pictures. For example, in his work known as the *Stromateis* ("Miscellanies," or literally, "patchwork") he draws from both testaments and the Apocrypha to describe the "mansions" of heaven:

There are various mansions according to the worth of the believers. Solomon says, "There shall be given to him the chosen grace of faith, and a more delightful portion in the temple of the Lord" [Wis. 3:14]. Here the comparative, "more delightful," indicates the lower portions of the Temple of God (which is the whole Church) but does not go as far as to include the superior division where the Lord is. That those three mansions are chosen abodes is the *hidden meaning* of the numbers in the gospel, "thirty, sixty, and a hundred" [Matthew 13:8; the reference is to the parable of the sower]. The perfect inheritance is theirs who attain "to the perfection of man" [Eph. 4:13], according to the Lord's image. (Clement, *Stromateis* VI, xiv; emphases added)

After Clement, by far the greatest hermeneut of the Alexandrian School is Origen (ca. 185–ca. 254), whose primarily allegorical reading of the Bible arises out of a theological contention "that the whole universe is pervaded with symbols and types of the invisible world. All things [have] a double aspect, one corporeal and sensible, which is accessible to all, the other spiritual and mystical, known only to the perfect" (*Oxford Dictionary of the Christian church*, 3d ed.). Thus, maintaining that there can be no salvation outside the church, Origen reads from Joshua 2 that "Rahab mystically represents the Church, the scarlet thread the blood of Christ, and only those in her house are saved." Origen sums up his reading of Scripture in this way. It is his answer to the question "What does the text *mean?*"

The Scriptures contain the ultimate mystery which can never be expressed other than in symbols and symbols can never be properly understood when taken literally. Therefore only an allegorical approach can provide the key, which is needed to unlock the mystery hidden in the text. (Origen, *Peri Archon* IV 2, 6, in Jeanrond, *Theological Hermeneutics*)

In the school of Antioch, however, whose hermeneuts also followed local Jewish traditions of interpretation, the emphasis was firmly on a primarily literal reading of the Bible and on the historical reality of its revelation. Readers like Theodore of Mopsuestia (ca. 350–428) rejected the notion of hidden meanings and regarded the Bible as clear and open to all who cared to read it. His concern was with careful textual and grammatical reading, and with a historical Christ "sprung from beneath" who shared in our humanity and raised it by moral means to the condition of the divine. For Theodore, reading the Old Testament from the New Testament is not an exercise in *typology* but *comparison*, and he denounces Origen and the Alexandrian scholars for their failure to understand that the Bible is *literally and historically true*. Thus in a ninth-century work entitled *Introduction to the Psalms* by Isho'-dad, which is based on the teachings of Theodore and described the Alexandrians as "stupid people," we read:

> The Psalms and the Prophets, who spoke of the captivity and return of the people, he [Origen] explained as teaching the captivity of the soul far from truth and its return to the faith. . . .They do not interpret paradise as it is, or Adam, or Eve, or any existing thing." (Quoted in Grant, *Short History of the Interpretation of the Bible*)

What we see here is that the way in which we read and interpret is dependent on the way in which we see the world and our place in it. This is as true for us as it was for these ancient Christian hermeneuts. We bring to the text our prior beliefs—whether they be of God or transcendence, or materialist and literal. For some of us the world is just the world, for others it is a sign and a symbol, a kind of window on a greater and other "reality."

5 Augustine, Bishop of Hippo (354–430)

By far the most important hermeneut of the early Christian church was Augustine, bishop of Hippo (354–430 C.E.), and we must confine ourselves to only the briefest sketch of his work here. Converted to Christianity in adult life—a process that is recounted in his most famous work, the *Confessions*—Augustine was well read in Greek and Platonic philosophy and, like Origen and others before him, he used this learning to good effect in his development of hermeneutical principles. Christian hermeneutics thus represents a mingling of Jewish and Greek traditions of reading and interpretation. Like Origen, Augustine developed sophisticated allegorical readings, as shown in Book XIII of the *Confessions*, an elaborate allegorical interpretation of the first chapter of Genesis. Here, for example, the darkness, which God divided from the light (v. 4), represents the soul still without God's light, while the plants given to humans for their food (v. 29) represent works of charity that nourish the soul. But, at the same time, Augustine developed manifold readings of Scripture, and no text is restricted to merely one exclusive "meaning." Indeed, he represents a resolution to the hermeneutical arguments between Alexandria and Antioch inasmuch as he developed a theory of interpretation that embraced both the literal and the allegorical or figurative perspectives, and in his treatise *On Christian Doctrine (De Doctrina Christiana)* Augustine proposes principles whereby a clear distinction between the two can be made. Within a given priority of spiritual praxis, the literal is always to be preferred, and so Augustine writes:

> With regard to figurative expressions the following rule should be observed; that what one reads should be carefully considered until a reading is established which reaches the kingdom of love. *But if the text sounds as if it is used in its proper* [literal] *sense, then the expression is not to be taken figuratively.* (Augustine, *De Doctrina Christiana* III, 23; emphasis added)

Augustine's greatest contribution to the development of hermeneutics is his "theory of signs" (or *semiotics*), which he expounds in *On Christian Doctrine*. In brief, for Augustine any reading of Scripture must be disciplined by a careful and thorough analysis of its language and grammatical structures in order to prevent wild and groundless exposition. Words are *signs*—that is, they refer to something as signifiers and are not to be confused with the thing to which they refer. As we shall see later, this is a remarkably modern insight into the nature of language. It is particularly important with respect to the Bible, because it leads Augustine actually to limit the role of Scripture, which he sees as human texts that refer to God but are not themselves to be regarded as in any sense divine. Thus the Bible is to be used as a guide to the Christian life, yet it is not absolutely essential, for there are other routes to salvation. Indeed, Augustine writes, "A person who bases his life firmly on faith, hope and love, thus needs the Scriptures only in order to teach others." Augustine was, after all, a bishop, and his hermeneutics reflect the thought of a practical person, not a remote academic. Indeed, although the Bible is, for him, the basis for the Christian life, he is not what the English poet Samuel Taylor Coleridge would later call a "bibliolater."

But we need to spend a little more time on the question of "signs." Although Augustine required his reader to be both intelligent and educated, for him the Bible was available in principle for all people to read and not just the theological elite, as became the case later, in the Middle Ages. We have seen how he recognized that words (or signs) can be either literal or figurative, and he set out principles for discerning the difference. But there is another problem for the reader for which Augustine offers help. We all know what it is to encounter a word that we either do not know or do not understand, or one that is ambiguous—that seems to suggest more than one meaning. Here Augustine anticipates later biblical criticism when he says that in seeking clarification, the reader must look to the broader context as well as the guidance of grammar. Words within a text cannot be understood in isolation. Finally, however, he follows earlier hermeneuts like Irenaeus and Tertullian in falling back on the final judgment of the rule of faith within the church, and this was later to ensure that in medieval Christendom the church maintained an iron grip on biblical hermeneutics, until Martin Luther and the Reformers recovered the wider aspects of Augustine's teaching.

Finally, in *De Doctrina* Augustine acknowledges that all reading is from a particular perspective. No reading is universal or "innocent." When reading the Bible we must adopt the perspective learned from the Bible itself—namely that of love, both of God and of our fellow human beings. As we shall see, this is repeated time and again up to the eighteenth century, in the insistence that we only read the Bible when we have said our prayers and put ourselves in the only frame of mind that will enable us truly to understand what we are reading. Interpreters from Aquinas to Erasmus, Luther, and even Schleiermacher (all of whom we shall consider) were at one in this. It was a principle broken only when the Enlightenment replaced love with reason as the proper perspective for the good reader. In his *Confessions*, Augustine realizes that he is unable to understand the Bible as long as his intellectual pride regards it as "inferior" to the stately prose of Cicero and the classical authors with whom he had been educated:

> For my swelling pride shrank from their lowliness, nor could my sharp wit pierce the interior thereof. Yet they were such as could grow up with little ones. But I disdained to be a little one, and swollen with pride, took myself to be a great one.
> (Augustine, *Confessions*)

We shall see later how learned German academics like Johann Gottfried Eichhorn (1752–1827) tended to regard the Scriptures as primitive writings. It is also useful to be reminded that proper understanding may require us sometimes to be content with the simple lest we are simply baffled by what seem to us clever and obscure arguments.

Augustine, then, anticipates much that we shall be encountering in our journey through the history of Western Christian hermeneutics, as well as insights in semiotics and linguistics that have only been recovered in recent times. Yet he was a curious mixture of blindness and insight, of intellectual perspicacity and cultural prejudice, as all of us are—though his perspicacity far outstripped what most of us can ever hope for. But by way of conclusion, read this passage from Augustine's great work *City of God* (Book XVII, chapter 20) on the relationship between the Old and the New Testaments. What do you think are its strengths and weaknesses? It is entitled "Psalm 69 Exposes the Unbelief and Obstinacy of the Jews" and bears close reading.

However, the Jews refuse to yield an inch in the face of such clear evidence as that of this prophecy, even when events have brought it so plainly and certainly to fulfillment; and therefore the words of the next psalm are, without question, fulfilled in them. For in that psalm also when the events connected with Christ's passion are being prophetically described, with Christ represented as the speaker, a detail is recorded whose meaning is revealed in the Gospel story, "They gave me gall to eat, and in my thirst they gave me vinegar to drink." Then after such a feast, as it were, and such a banquet had been offered to him, he went on to say, "Let their table become a trap before them, and a retribution and a snare. May their eyes be dimmed so that they may not see, and their backs always bowed. . . ." This was not said by way of a wish; it was a prophetic prediction in the form of a wish. Is it any wonder, then, if those whose eyes were dimmed to prevent their seeing fail to observe these obvious facts? Is it any wonder if those whose backs are always bowed so that they bend down toward things of earth, fail to look upwards toward things in heaven? For these bodily metaphors refer to spiritual things.

But this discussion must be kept within bounds, and so let this suffice for my treatment of the psalms, that is of the prophecy of King David. I hope that my readers who are familiar with the whole subject will forgive me, and will not complain if they know or suppose that I have passed over other passages which perhaps provide stronger evidence. (Augustine, *City of God*)

Summary

We might summarize the main points of this chapter as follows:

1. Ancient Jewish interpreters had a different understanding of text and reader; the Torah as the blueprint of creation.
2. There are hermeneutics *in* the Bible itself; the Bible as an edited and translated text.

3. There are typological and christological readings of the Hebrew Bible in the New Testament.
4. The establishment of the "canon" of the Christian Bible, and the *regula veritatis*, or "canon of truth," was long and debated.
5. In Antioch, Scripture reading inclined to be literal; in Alexandria, allegorical or figurative.
6. Augustine's theory of semiotics contributed to the stabilizing of Christian hermeneutics.

Activities and Questions

1. We usually think of reading as a rather solitary activity. For the ancient Rabbis, however, reading was actually profoundly sociable and the "pretext" for conversation, argument, and debate. Texts were not conclusive, but open-ended and discursive. Try to find some examples of contemporary "midrashic" literature that have these qualities that stimulate conversation, rather than the "Aristotelian" qualities of order and conclusion. You might find them in poetry or drama, but perhaps also in theological or even philosophical works. Make brief comments on them.
2. Find three examples of *typological* readings of the Hebrew Bible in the New Testament apart from the ones given in this chapter.
3. The debate over the Christian canon—which texts were to be included and which were not—raises the question, What are the criteria for calling a text "sacred"? What do you think about this? (Remember the odd ideas put forward by Irenaeus to establish the canonicity of the four Gospels.)
4. What are the respective hermeneutical merits and demerits of the "schools" of Antioch and Alexandria?
5. Why are semiotics so important for hermeneutics? (Remember how much we depend on the *stability* of language to communicate with one another. If signs, or words, are not themselves what they refer to, how can we guarantee *anything* that we say?)

Chapter Three

From Scholasticism to the Age of Enlightenment

1 Medieval Hermeneutics: Thomas Aquinas (ca. 1225–74)

Of necessity our story will be selective and compressed, as time will later be devoted to more detailed examinations of recent developments in hermeneutical thinking over the last two hundred years. However, it is very important to have some sense of the *continuity* of hermeneutics from the earliest Christian times, with which we have so far largely been concerned. The story is a connected one, although at the same time one of continuous change as evolving worldviews shifted the way people not only saw the world but actually thought and, therefore, read.

The medieval church in the West, at least until the thirteenth century, more or less followed the hermeneutics of Augustine and the Fathers. Although the subtlety and variety of the early hermeneuts were often lost as "authorities" were cited in lists designed to solidify the "norm of the ecclesiastical and catholic sense," and the Greek fathers like Clement and Origen tended to be subordinated to the Latin tradition, *continuity* was maintained without much innovative thought, though with one great distorting factor. The church as an institution grew ever more mighty and wielded power that was not only theological and spiritual, but also political. Indeed, its influence spread over every aspect of people's lives. Augustine had been profoundly concerned with the business of *reading* and interpreting texts, and above all the Bible. Increasingly in the Middle Ages, however, the theology and the theological speculation of the church tended to be separated from the processes of biblical interpretation, and *sacra scriptura* became merely the proof of the truth of *sacra doctrina*. Any textual divergence from the sacred doctrines of the church was liable to be consigned to the flames as heretical. To read was largely a matter of following order and remaining faithful to the tradition handed down. At the same time, under the recovery of learning associated with the emperor Charlemagne (ca. 742–814), sometimes known as the Carolingian revival, *glosses* or marginal commentaries, called *sententiae*, on the texts of Scripture, often in the form of theological questions, came to assume as great an importance as the text of the Bible itself. Later on this was to be one of the preoccupations of Martin Luther, who wanted to throw away such "commentaries" and reintroduce the reader simply to the text itself. But in the Middle Ages, theology took its place as the queen of sciences.

Biblical hermeneutics, however, as pursued in monasteries and other places of learning, actually diverged little from the lead given by the early church fathers. Still, in one respect medieval interpreters were very similar to Martin Luther and the later hermeneuts of the Reformation: that is, in their emphasis on the reader's prior *disposition* when reading the Bible. They insisted that when reading Scripture you must *first* be in a right spiritual frame of mind and spirit. Say your prayers, pledge your allegiance to the church, and only *then* can you read the sacred text. Here is a hermeneutics of faith with a vengeance! If the modern hermeneut sharpens his or her critical and even skeptical faculties in order to ensure a right reading, the medieval reader fell to his (or, much more rarely in that age, her) knees first.

In other respects, these medieval scholars followed the traditional methods of the church in more than one way—indeed, in basically four ways, which they called the *literal*, the *allegorical*, the *moral*, and the *anagogical*. (This last term, *anagogical*, is derived from Greek and means generally religious, spiritual, or often mystical. It refers here to an understanding of spiritual mysteries and, therefore, to the mystery of the end of human life.) These four ways of reading are described in a verse of Nicholas of Lyra (ca. 1270–1349), a French Franciscan scholar:

> The *letter* shows us what God and our fathers did;
> The *allegory* shows us where our faith is hid;
> The *moral* meaning gives us rules of daily life;
> The *anagogy* shows us where we end our strife.
>
> (Quoted in Jeanrond, *Theological Hermeneutics*)

Scripture offers not just one meaning, and there is more than one way to read the Bible, which yields its riches on these many levels. It teaches us history. It gives us insight into the mystery of faith and belief. It guides us in the moral conduct of our lives each day. Finally, it indicates the nature of our end and the fulfillment of all things in God. Thus, on the one hand, if we followed Nicholas of Lyra, reading Scripture was an activity, or rather a series of activities, that governed every aspect of life. On the other hand, however, this division of different kinds of reading also tended to separate out different disciplines within the "science" of theology, and ultimately had the effect of actually depreciating the status of the biblical text itself.

This is most clearly seen in the work of the greatest of all medieval theologians, or scholastics, Thomas Aquinas. At the heart of Aquinas's project is one word—*reason*. When he used the word, however, it was not in quite the same way as we do. "Reason" for Aquinas was thinking in conformity with the mind of God—it was God-centered and not, as it was later to become, human-centered and based on the faculties of the human mind. But still, for Aquinas, theology was a science and an academic business, summed up in his great work the *Summa theologica*. Alongside the speculative exercise of theology, biblical texts become simply proofs, to be read literally. Allegorical readings tended to vanish in the face of the new academic theology (though not in sermons and preaching), while medieval interpreters happily provided their *sententiae* or "glosses," thus frequently submerging the text itself under the weight of their own "scientific" explanations. It was certainly *not* the case that Aquinas did not take the Bible seriously. Quite to the contrary. The problem with allegorical interpretations was that they tended to be too subjective (and often found more in medieval preaching), while Aquinas, devoted to philosophical understanding, acknowledged that the Bible is the primary source of revelation and is free from error. This he writes at the beginning of his *Summa theologica*:

> Sacred doctrine makes use also of the authority of philosophers in those questions in which they were able to know the truth by natural reason, as Paul quotes a saying of Aratus [Acts 17:28]. Nevertheless, sacred doctrine makes use of these authorities as extrinsic and probable arguments, *but properly uses the authority of the scriptures as incontrovertible proof* (Aquinas, *Summa theologica*; emphasis added)

Yet Aquinas does not finally abandon allegorical readings of the Bible, and always in his philosophical and essentially rational mind the tendency was for the Scriptures to become *pretexts* for the real business and purpose of hermeneutics, which was the teaching and doctrine of the church.

2   Two Medieval Minds: Meister Eckhart and Thomas à Kempis

At the same time, as is often the case and is certainly so today, there was a broad split between the learning of the academy and popular piety in the medieval church, and those associated with the latter read the Bible in a rather different way from the former. It is far from the case that popular piety and religion are without hermeneutics, and they may indeed be as sophisticated in their own way as the learned interpretive strategies of the universities. Indeed, *all* reading presupposes hermeneutics of some kind. As we have seen, the ancient allegorical readings of Scripture survived largely in preaching. And so, in two examples of more "popular" medieval readings of the Bible, we turn first to a preacher. Here is an excerpt from a sermon by the radical mystical thinker and preacher Meister Eckhart (ca. 1260–ca. 1327), which is notable because it comes to us in German rather than Latin—that is, in the vernacular, although admittedly it is a rather high-flown form of German. Eckhart's text is Luke 10:38–40, about Jesus' visit to the house of Martha and Mary:

> Now as they went on their way, he entered a certain village, where a woman named Martha welcomed him into her home. She had a sister named Mary, who sat at the Lord's feet and listened to what he was saying. But Martha was distracted by her many tasks.

Here is how Meister Eckhart reads this passage:

> St Luke writes in his Gospel that our Lord entered a small town where he was received by a woman called Martha. She had a sister, whose name was Mary. Mary sat at the feet of our Lord and listened to his words, while Martha moved about and waited on our Lord.
>
> Now there are three things, which caused Mary to sit at the feet of our Lord. The first was that the goodness of God has seized her soul. The second was an inexpressible desire: she was filled with longing, but did not know what for. She was filled with desire, but did not know why. The third thing was the sweet consolation and the bliss that came to her from the eternal words, which flowed from the mouth of Christ.
>
> There were three things too, which caused Martha to move about and to serve her beloved Christ. The first was her maturity and the ground of her being, which she had trained to the greatest extent and which, she believed, qualified her best of all to undertake these tasks. The second was wise understanding which knew how to perform those works

perfectly that love commands. And the third was the particular honour of her precious guest. (Eckhart, Sermon 21, in *Selected Writings*)

You see how Eckhart here is a good medieval theologian while at the same time appealing to a congregation seeking to make sense of Scripture for their lives, rather than a learned reader of the Bible who is searching for philosophical and theological enlightenment. Eckhart's method is what we call *eisegesis* rather than *exegesis*—that is, a reading *into (eis-)* the text rather than a reading *out of* or *from (ex-)* the text. Still, like Aquinas, he begins with elegantly balanced speculation, doctrine, and moral teaching and brings these to the text, which then becomes a sort of ground where they are tested. To us it may seem a little odd, and we are tempted to retort, "But this is not what the text *says*. How does he know that these are the things which caused Mary and Martha to behave in the ways that they did?" To us it seems hardly a careful reading, and what is to prevent him from bringing more or less anything he likes into the text? Of course that is right, and in one sense Eckhart *is* reading things into the text, but the point is that that is precisely what he intends to do, for, from his spiritual perspective, as Werner Jeanrond puts it, "the texts were increasingly reduced to providers of proofs for speculative theological thought ventures." (Jeanrond, *Theological Hermeneutics*)

About one hundred years later, at the very end of the Middle Ages, another German, Thomas à Kempis, (ca. 1380–1471), wrote his hugely influential devotional work *De Imitatione Christi* (*The Imitation of Christ*), or, at least, so it is generally believed. His purpose is the practical one of instructing the Christian on how to seek perfection by following Christ as the model of life and living life in the imitation of Christ. Chapter 5 of the *Imitation* is entitled "On Reading the Holy Scriptures." It is very brief. Here is the chapter in full:

In the Holy Scriptures, truth is to be looked for rather than fair phrases. All sacred scriptures should be read in the spirit in which they were written. In them therefore we should seek food for our souls rather than subtleties of speech, and we should as readily read simple and devout books as those that are lofty and profound. Do not be influenced by the importance of the writer, and whether his learning be great or small, but let the love of pure truth draw you to read. Do not inquire, "Who said this?" But pay attention to what is said. Men pass away, but the word of the Lord endures forever. God speaks to us in different ways, and is no respecter of persons. But curiosity often hinders us in the reading of the Scriptures, for we try to examine and dispute over matters that we should pass over and accept in simplicity. If you desire to profit, read with humility, simplicity, and faith and have no concern to appear learned. Ask questions freely, and listen in silence to the words of the Saints; hear with patience the parables of the fathers, for they are not told without good cause. (Thomas à Kempis, *The Imitation of Christ*)

The stress here is on simplicity rather than learning, and on a *literal* reading rather than the high-flown speculations of allegorical or "difficult" interpretation. In many respects, Thomas à Kempis anticipates the Protestant Reformers who came shortly after him, while at the same time he is not so far from Thomas Aquinas. For him, reading the Bible is not to indulge in flights of learning, but rather a "paying attention" and an exercise in *listening* to the saints and the "fathers"—that is, the fathers of the church, through whom God speaks. You see how he remains a good medieval. To the Bible is still added the *catena*, or collections, of interpretations of the early fathers. Furthermore, there is no one correct way of reading, but many, and each reader "hears" the word in the way intended for him or her. This brief "chapter" from this widely read work is a fascinating moment in which medieval hermeneutics are beginning to make way for the hermeneutics of the Reformation, with their emphasis on the individual listening with humble simplicity to the word of God in Scripture. Of course, the Reformation was never quite that simple—as, by now, you might expect, and as we shall see!

3   Christian Humanism:
Desiderius Erasmus (1466/9–1536)

The Dutch humanist Erasmus of Rotterdam is also a pivotal figure who looks both backward to the medieval world and forward to the Reformation and the modern world. A deeply learned scholar, he followed the Greek Platonist tradition of Augustine of Hippo. He read carefully and critically the works of the early church fathers (but not just in the medieval *catena*), and read the Bible itself with a mixture of literal and allegorical understandings. At the same time he was vastly learned in classical literature, both Latin and Greek, and was one of the first people to insist on a "correct" and scholarly text of the Bible, producing one of the first critically edited versions of the New Testament in Greek using different manuscripts, and with his own translation into classical Latin. Although this edition was deficient in many respects, in it Erasmus foreshadowed the modern scholarship that seeks to establish as nearly as possible the text "as it was written." A humanist who could be scathing and even irreverent in his own writings (such as in his best-known work, *The Praise of Folly*), Erasmus was a controversial figure who earned the hatred of, among others in the church, the Spanish Inquisition. Learning, it seems, is always a dangerous thing!

Erasmus's insistence on establishing the proper text of the New Testament by applying scholarly principles to the editing of variant readings in different manuscripts sprang from a belief in the Bible as the revealed Word of God and our duty to attend to that Word as exactly as possible. Reading the Bible was, for Erasmus, a kind of exchange between the text and the reader, which brings about a transformation in the reader as its mysteries are revealed in the process of reading. This is actually quite a revolutionary change in the understanding of Scripture, for the emphasis is now shifting from Scripture as "proof text" for theology and the tradition, to an acknowledgment of the importance of that moment of exchange in the act of reading itself. This is a dynamic and interactive process, both vital and of the moment, and Erasmus fiercely criticized the "coldness" of earlier medieval interpreters. It was, we might say, an early instance of what we would now call *reader-*

response criticism, a term that we have already encountered in chapter 1.

Unlike Thomas à Kempis, Erasmus encourages us to be learned readers, for, as he said, "knowledge or learning fortifies the mind," and by this he means something much more "modern" than we have encountered so far. Erasmus was, undoubtedly, a widely read man, and that, he believes, is a good thing in itself. At the same time, Scripture must still be read with a prayerful attitude and with a disposition given to faith and reverence. This is still a hermeneutics of faith. However, our wider reading is not to be restricted, said Erasmus, simply to the sacred texts of the Bible. From the pre-Christian classical authors such as Homer (in Greek) and Virgil (in Latin), to the careful reading of the church fathers such as Jerome (the learned and irascible translator of the Bible into the Latin *Vulgate* form) and Augustine, he insists, we can derive great benefits, provided we are careful to avoid "obscene passages." Here, interestingly, we are beginning to see the distinction that the Reformation was to establish firmly between *sacred* and *secular* literature, though Erasmus is far more broad-minded than Luther. But he does raise the thorny question of what (or who) exactly defines a term such as "obscene" and who legitimates what we read. Is it the church, in all its authority, or can the individual reader be trusted to discriminate for himself or herself, or are there general hermeneutical principles that we can rely on to guide us? In the end, Erasmus seems to suggest, something is obscene if it bothers us as such. If it does not, presumably we are at liberty to read it. This remains today a very difficult question, still open to debate, as we shall see in chapter 7 of this book. (As a sneak preview you might look up T. S. Eliot's 1935 essay "Religion and Literature," reprinted in his *Selected Essays,* which seeks to stabilize by recourse to a "definite ethical and theological

> As a sneak preview you might look up T. S. Eliot's 1935 essay "Religion and Literature," reprinted in his *Selected Essays,* which seeks to stabilize by recourse to a "definite ethical and theological standpoint" the very boat that Erasmus seems to be rocking—how successfully you need to decide for yourself.

standpoint" the very boat that Erasmus seems to be rocking—how successfully you need to decide for yourself.)

Here is a crucial passage from Erasmus's work the *Enchiridion militis Christiani* (*The Handbook of the Militant Christian*), published in 1503 with the intent to promote a practical Christianity, partly through a reading of the classics, but finally based on a firmly evangelical knowledge of Scripture as the Word of Christ. Here we have clearly moved out of the world of medieval glosses and biblical proof texts. It is of necessity a long quotation, for Erasmus is best left to speak for himself.

> You must believe when I say that there is really no attack from the enemy, no temptation so violent that a sincere resort to Holy Writ will not easily get rid of it. There is no misfortune so sad that a reading of the scriptures does not render bearable. Therefore if you will but dedicate yourself entirely to the study of the scriptures, if you meditate day and night on the divine law, nothing will ever terrorize you and you will be prepared against any attack of the enemy.
>
> I might also add that a sensible reading of the pagan poets and philosophers is a good preparation for the Christian life. We have the example of St. Basil, who recommends the ancient poets for their natural goodness. Both St. Augustine and St. Jerome followed this method. St. Cyprian has worked wonders in adorning the Scriptures with the literary beauty of the ancients. Of course it is not my intention that you imbibe the bad morals of the pagans along with their literary excellence. I am sure that you will nonetheless find many examples in the classics that are conducive to right living. Many of these writers were, of course, very good teachers of ethics. We have the example of Moses, who did not spurn the advice of Jethro. These readings mature us and constitute a wonderful preparation for an understanding of the Scriptures. I feel this is quite important, because to break in upon these sacred writings without this preparation is almost sacrilegious. St. Jerome assails the presumption of those who, even though they may be learned in other fields, presume to

expatiate on the Bible. You can imagine the audacity of those who, having no preparation whatsoever, try to do the same thing.

We must not persist in clinging to the letter, and the reading of Homer and Virgil will be of no use unless we look to its allegorical side. If you like the classics, then you will understand what I mean. If the obscene passages in the ancients bother you, then by all means refrain from reading them. Of all the philosophical writings I would recommend the Platonists most highly. For not only their ideas but also their very mode of expression approaches that of the Gospels. Of course they should be read in a cursory manner, and whatever is of real value in them should be applied and referred to Christ. If to the pure of heart all things are clean, then to the impure everything appears to be unclean. Whenever the reading of the secular selections arouses your baser appetites, then leave them alone.

Reading the scriptures with a clean heart is a basic rule.
(Erasmus, *Enchiridion*, in *The Essential Erasmus*)

This passage provides a fascinating development from the kind of medieval hermeneutics that we have seen earlier. Erasmus still reads the church fathers, but appeals to them as authorities while also allowing us to read the "pagan" authors along with the Bible. In reading Homer and Virgil we should not "cling to the letter," but have resort to allegorical interpretations, presumably as people had been wont to do with such an obviously erotic text in the Bible as the Song of Solomon. Above all, notice how Erasmus uses the Bible itself to provide the authority and establish the principles he is arguing for. The example of Moses and Jethro does seem to justify the reading of "pagan" writers. And where do we find guidance in the discrimination between what is acceptable and what is not? In the first instance we find it in Scripture; "to the pure of heart all things are clean" (and see also Mark 7:14–23), and from that we can take our cue. How do we best read and especially best read the Bible? The answer is: read the Bible to find out.

Note also how Erasmus commends not only the "ideas" in classical texts, such as those of Homer and Virgil, but also their "mode of expression." *How* a text says something is as important as *what* it says, and so his hermeneutics acknowledges the question of *aesthetics*, or literary form and beauty, in the processes of interpretation. This is something we have not really encountered before, and it is an early version of what in our own time the Canadian scholar Marshall McLuhan has promoted through the catch phrase "The medium is the message." Or, to put it even more simply, in texts it is not just *what* you do, it is *the way* that you do it.

4   Martin Luther (1483–1536) and John Calvin (1509–64)

The Protestant Reformation, which finally erupted in the sixteenth century, first in Germany (although its roots go back much farther than that) affected the greatest revolution in hermeneutics (apart from anything else) that the church in the West has known. Here we can barely scrape the surface of its complexity and indicate some of the ways in which, as readers of texts, we still owe an enormous dept to the debates of those times. Their concerns were theological, but in many ways they changed quite radically how we read, interpret, understand, and *use* texts of every kind and not just the Bible.

My first point may seem a little surprising, but it is important. Martin Luther's hermeneutical enterprise was partly made possible by an advance in technology, that is, the invention of the *printing press*. As we saw in chapter 1, changes in hermeneutics and technological developments often go hand in hand, as the latter effectively change the world in which we live and the ways in which we perceive it. In print the hand of humankind was literally extended, and the modern world was entered on. Luther was a university lecturer, and for the first time, by courtesy of the printing press, he could rely on all his students having before them a text of the Bible that was standard and easily available. Books were no longer subject to the vagaries of scribal copying. However careful we are, we all know how easy it is to make mistakes in the simple act of copying a text. No longer was this now the case. Each text of the Bible was exactly the same as all others. Futhermore, books were also increasingly widely available and not restricted to single, precious copies locked away in churches or in libraries. The result was the spread of literacy, even among people of modest means and little formal learning, and thus began the growth of vernacular Bibles in English, German, French, and so on. Thus we find Erasmus saying in his *Exhortations to the Diligent Study of Scripture* (1529), in the English translation of one of the great translators of the English Bible, William Tyndale: "I wold to god the plowman wold singe a text of the scripture at his plowbeme, and that the weaver at his lowme with this wold drive away the tediousness of tyme."

The Bible now might be the property of every man, even in his common labor, and might climb away from the restrictions of the study and the cloister. But we must not be too hasty. Luther, like Erasmus, was as much a medieval scholar as he was a reformer, and he was well trained in medieval, scholastic theology. To begin with, he read the Bible with a sense of the old fourfold meaning, but gradually came to reject allegorical and analogical readings, retorting, "I know they are nothing but rubbish." Nor was his reason for this anything like that of the learned Thomas Aquinas, for Luther's concern was to set the Bible free to interact with the subjective experience of the reader, not to substantiate the theology of the church. Although his work is never entirely consistent (Luther was not a particularly tidy thinker), his basic interest came to be in the literal and *tropological*, or moral, sense of Scripture. In his criticism of the power and corruption of the church as an institution, Luther insists that the Bible was the sole criterion and arbiter of tradition, appealing to the "plain" or "natural" meaning of the text. Concentrating on historical and grammatical principles of interpretation and on exegesis, Luther's regard for the traditions of the church fathers was not because they provided any authoritative or even legal inheritance, but only insofar as they were themselves competent hermeneuts. The reader alone confronts the text, without the intervention of the church and its theology, and seeks to avoid "multiple" meanings. In his classes at the University of Wittenberg in 1513–14, Luther insisted that each of his students have a copy of the text for personal reference. We might say that this was the first "modern" class, and his advice to his class was clear: "Experience is necessary for the understanding of the Word. It is not merely to be repeated or known, but to be lived and felt."

The key word is "experience," that is, not a knowledge of theology or the church's teachings. Luther did not read the Bible primarily as a historical record—that was an issue that was to become crucial in hermeneutics only much later, in the eighteenth century. His reading was firmly *christological* and undeniably subjective. To put this more plainly, the words of Scripture are Christ speaking to the reader, the very words of Christ himself. This is true even for the books of the Old Testament, although his emphasis is clearly on certain books of the New Testament, and in particular Paul's letters to the Romans and Galatians, the Gospel of John, and the First Letter of Peter. (Luther's tendencies toward anti-Semitism are, it has to be admitted, notorious.) Nevertheless, in Luther's hermeneutics the "I" of the psalms is the actual voice of Christ himself speaking to each of us. Thus, in short, to read the Bible is to come to Christ himself, who speaks to the individual as he or she faces and is faced by the text, and, he insists, "There is not on earth a book more lucidly written than the Holy Scripture."

But still we should not imagine that reading the Bible is an easy task, and Luther offers us no shortcuts through the necessary thickets and brambles of interpretation. He remains the schoolmaster and reminds us in the preface to his commentary on Isaiah that the reader needs to be equipped with a clear historical understanding of the origins of the text and its author. (One wonders a little how possible this is for the working plowman busy at his plow or the weaver at his loom!) Not least, we have to acknowledge our own limitations as interpreters, and our own capacity for misunderstanding. What Luther offers us is not a conclusive exercise, but a way to proceed, and Luther is far from later tendencies in Lutheran thinking toward biblical fundamentalism and an absolute, unintellectual faith in verbal inspiration.

Yet the principle of *sola scriptura* (Scripture alone) is firmly established. Ultimately no other authority or commentary is necessary, for Scripture is its own interpreter—*scriptura scripturae interpres* (Scripture the interpreter of Scripture)—and it is the source of *all* interpretation. Luther writes:

> This is the true touchstone by which all books are to be judged, when one sees whether they urge Christ or not, as all scripture shows forth Christ, and St. Paul will know no-one but Christ [1 Corinthians 2:2]. (Quoted in Grant, *Short History of the Interpretation of the Bible*)

As we read we begin with the literal sense, and from this a spiritual understanding will grow as the text *discloses* or reveals the Word of God. (We need to be clear that for Luther the Bible is not simply the Word of God, as such, but rather a way of gaining access to it. For this reason his own translation of it into German is often quite free almost to the point of paraphrase.) We must apply ourselves to the task of interpretation, and slowly our sense of the world will be transformed with Christ providing a unifying focus to the contradictions of the text. (Luther was well aware that the Bible is not always consistent and often actually contradicts itself.)

For Luther, as for Erasmus and all earlier Christian hermeneuts, the *disposition* of the reader remains crucial: we must preface our reading with prayer and continue with the eye of faith, and our faith is thereby strengthened by our reading. But although his is clearly a hermeneutics of faith, it is also actually a hermeneutics of suspicion, at least in principle, for thereby we grow in faith in a typically circular movement from universal faith to particular inquiry and back to universal faith, which is strengthened in the process.

We need to recognize also that for Luther, Scripture interprets us as much as we interpret Scripture. Here is Luther himself, speaking in the *Table Talk*. Compare this carefully with the quotation given a few pages ago from Erasmus's *Enchiridion*:

> The Holy Scriptures are full of divine gifts and virtues. The books of the heathen taught nothing of faith, hope, or charity; they present no idea of these things; they contemplate only the present, and that which man, with the use of his material reason, can grasp and comprehend. Look not therein for aught of hope or trust in God. But see how the Psalms and the Book of Job treat of faith, hope, resignation, and prayer; in a word, the Holy Scripture is the highest and best of books, abounding in comfort under all afflictions and trials. It teaches us to see, to feel, to grasp, and to comprehend faith, hope, and charity, far otherwise than mere human reason can; and when evil oppresses us, it teaches how these virtues throw light upon the darkness, and how, after this poor, miserable existence of ours on earth, there is another and an eternal life.
>
> We ought not to criticize, explain, or judge the Scriptures by our mere reason, but diligently, with prayer, meditate thereon, and seek their meaning. The devil and temptations also afford us occasion to learn and understand the Scriptures, by experience and practice.
>
> Without these we should never understand them, however diligently we read and listened to them. The Holy Ghost must be our only master and tutor; and let youth have no shame to learn of that preceptor. When I find myself assailed by temptation, I forth-with lay hold of some text of the Bible, which Jesus extends to me; as this: that he died for me, whence I derive infinite hope. (Luther, *Table Talk* 2, 4)

Luther is as interested as Aquinas in theology, but for him theology *begins and ends* with the Bible alone, beyond all mere "reason."

John Calvin of Geneva is the other great figure of the Reformation. Trained as a lawyer, his mind was much more organized than Luther's and, despite the often dour rigors of what came to be known as *Calvinism*, more adapted to the tradition of humanist learning such as we found in Erasmus. Calvin's reading of the Bible is grounded in rational reflection, self-understanding, and common sense, for he affirmed, "Without knowledge of ourselves, knowledge of God does not take place." His reader is less of an individual than is the case with Luther, but interprets within the context of society while at the same time bringing to the text his or her own creative imagination. Furthermore, if Luther begins with a christological interpretation, Calvin, with his legal mind, relies on exegesis of Scripture confirmed by the "internal testimony of the Holy Spirit." And if Luther would give the Bible to everyone, Calvin is clear that faith is not given to all. It is not given to everyone to understand the words of Scripture.

Calvin, too, has his own hermeneutic circle. A modern commentator on him, Christopher Elwood, has put it in this way:

> But how do we know God speaks in Scripture? We know it because we experience God speaking in Scripture. That is, we become certain that Scripture is God's word to us when God's spirit testifies to us, or confirms to us that this is God's word. Here Calvin's reasoning seems to be circular, but the circularity is not unintentional. To try to establish the authority of the Bible by adducing proofs or by appealing to some criteria outside of God's word to us would be to create another authority higher than Scripture, an authority on which we would then have to depend for trusting that we hear God when we read the Bible. But Scripture doesn't need any external proof. (Elwood, *Calvin for Armchair Theologians*)

There is nothing outside the text, it seems. By a curious set of circumstances, modern, or perhaps postmodern, literary theory has come to the same conclusion, as we shall see later, though there God is left out of the equation and the text becomes *self-authenticating*. But still there is an odd hermeneutical similarity between Calvin and the contemporary French thinker Jacques Derrida, whom we shall come to in chapter 6.

Finally, Calvin anticipates another huge hermeneutical issue when he places the Bible in a historical context, for the reader must appreciate not only his or her own mind but also the *very mind of the biblical author*, that is, in the writing of the text prior to the theology and authority of the church. This principle also we will return to in chapter 4 when we come to consider the work of Friedrich Schleiermacher in the early nineteenth century. I mention this only to indicate that in the history of hermeneutics we keep coming back to the same issues in different guises and under changed circumstances. There is, indeed, nothing new under the sun!

5 The Age of Reason

We can see already in the great Reformers a shift away from Augustine's worldview to a perspective on things that was to change our whole outlook on reality and how we understand ourselves and the world. Hermeneutics, too, changed radically. How we read is dependent on the way we see and understand the world: whether, for example, we believe that God does or does not exist. Given the sort of men Luther and Calvin were, both deeply religious, the hermeneutical shift that they in many ways initiated has a certain irony, for it was actually away from a worldview that was utterly God-centered, or *theocentric*, to one that is human-centered, or *anthropocentric*. The reason for this was that, however much they tried to avoid and deny it, their hermeneutics opened up the way for subjectivism and the mind of the individual reader, and therefore for the claims of the human mind to be the prior faculty in the interpretation of texts, even the text of the Bible itself.

The first great philosopher of the "age of reason" is the Frenchman René Descartes (1596–1650), whose famous Latin adage *cogito ergo sum* ("I think, therefore I am") set the seal on modernity with its clear division between the sacred and the secular realms, its increasing anxiety about the very being of God and even God's existence, and its faith in the capacity of human reason and logic to understand for itself without divine guidance. In short, we no longer need to say our prayers before we begin to read the Bible. We can start, as it were, with an open mind. We can now interpret, define ourselves, and indeed our very existence and the world in which we live, by our capacity to think quite independently of God. Augustine, if he could even have understood this, would have been utterly horrified, as indeed would every interpreter whom we have encountered so far.

As an example of the consequences of this radical shift in human self-awareness for hermeneutics, we will briefly consider the German scholar Johann Martin Chladenius (1710–59), who was for the last years of his life professor of theology, rhetoric, and poetry at the University of Erlangen. Although he was the son of an eminent theologian, as a scholar Chladenius was not primarily interested in theology, nor even particularly in the Bible. This alone sets him apart from every hermeneut whom we have studied so far. Instead, he was concerned with the theoretical study of interpretation of texts—all texts—as an end in itself. His rather cumbersomely entitled book *Introduction to the Correct Interpretation of Reasonable Discourses and Writings* (1742) is one of the first systematic treatises on hermeneutics as a branch of study in itself, and not as an end in a primarily religious, theological, or even ethical exercise. Hermeneutics has now become something like a *secular* discipline in the academy, perhaps more closely linked to philosophy than to theology. Note the presence of the word "reasonable" in the title of his book. For Chladenius, "reason" in the modern sense of the word (related to the human mind), and not as Aquinas understood it (related to the mind of God), lies at the heart of every proper interpretive investigation.

According to Chladenius, the purpose of a text and the act of reading that it requires and provokes is "complete understanding." We must finally be left with no loose ends or vague areas. Our primary tools to bring about this understanding are a reasonable mind and common sense. Most importantly, we should be from the very start wary readers. "One should doubt all things once," Chladenius insisted. Take nothing on faith. Here is a *hermeneutics of suspicion* with a vengeance! To take anything on trust, or in faith, is for Chladenius both unreasonable and most unwise. Nevertheless, he freely admits, complete understanding is difficult and complex and is possible only after a great deal of effort and on the basis of careful investigation. He admits that finding the right way is often a matter of trial and error, and the best thing may be to find an experienced teacher, "someone who fully understands the book and knows which concepts we need to acquire." He is the university professor to the core, with an unquestioning respect for scholarship!

Chladenius, it has to be admitted, is not an exciting thinker, although he is useful to us because he is very much a man of his times. In his dry, academic hands "reading" becomes a science to be approached rationally and scientifically and with every expectation of an ultimately clear and correct outcome. All misrepresentations of a text must be ultimately willful and against reason. In the end, he states quite categorically, "an interpretation has to be correct." But it is interesting to note that when he comes to the interpretation of the Bible, Chladenius makes an important distinction. Here is a passage from chapter 4 of the *Introduction to Correct Interpretation*:

> Theology relies primarily on the interpretation of Holy Scripture. For this reason, much effort has been made over the course of many years to collect rules suitable for its interpretation. Hermeneutics would stand itself in good stead here to acknowledge that it alone does not determine the matter. The Holy Scriptures are a work of God for which many rules might be more certain than for human books. However, many rules which might be useful here, cannot be applied at all. Revelation has its own special criticism, which goes beyond this—there are secrets and prophecies which we are led to, not through philosophy, but through revelation. It is a book which is written for the whole world and it has its own special consequences for the interpretation which can only be introduced in a work of God. The usefulness of the general rules for the interpretation of the Holy Scriptures will reveal itself when these have become better known and more precise with time. (Quoted in Kurt Mueller-Vollmer, ed., *The Hermeneutics Reader*)

Clearly Chladenius still stands somewhat uncomfortably within the Protestant tradition, seeing the Bible as the source of theology, and for once his logical mind slips into a rather inconsequential, even slightly embarrassed, argument. What is clear in this passage is that there are different sets of rules for interpreting the Bible, on the one hand, and interpreting all other books, on the other. The sacred Scriptures stand apart, different in nature as text because they are a "work of God." This distinction between sacred and secular texts had been implicit in earlier hermeneutics, but never so fully stated in such a clear way before. It suggests that there are actually *two* kinds of hermeneutics, one for the Bible and the other (which is really what Chladenius is concerned with), for all other texts. The dangers this rift opened up are either of a biblical fundamentalism, which simply abandons serious hermeneutical questions in the reading of Scripture, or of the impossibility of reading the Bible at all, leaving it beached and irrelevant on the shores of the rest of world literature. The fact that Chladenius still regards the Bible (for whatever reason is not clear) as "a work of God" results in "its own special consequences for interpretation," and basically he prefers to ignore it altogether. Thus the march of reason in hermeneutics poses a serious threat to the traditional *authority* of the Bible, unless you opt to suspend reason altogether and read by faith alone. But now, as never before, you had a choice—between the sacred and the secular paths. There are, in effect, two kinds of hermeneutics.

Summary

We might summarize the main points of this chapter as follows:

1. Medieval hermeneutics is in essential continuity with the hermeneutics of the Fathers of the early church.
2. Thomas Aquinas and the scholastic tradition pursue a speculative theology, the Bible providing proof texts. The interpretation of Scripture is essentially separated from the study of theology.
3. Meister Eckhart as a preacher reads the Bible by an exercise in *eisegesis* rather than *exegesis*. Thomas à Kempis sees reading

the Scriptures as a "listening" to the divine voice on the way
to an imitation of Christ.

4. With the new power of printing, Luther encourages everyone to read for themselves, illuminated by the principle of *sola
   scriptura*. Unlike the humanist Erasmus, Luther discouraged
   the reading of other literature besides the Bible.

5. Chladenius subsumes all under the direction of human *reason*—but an exception is made for the Bible as the "work of
   God." Scripture is thus isolated from other literature.

6. We now must choose between a hermeneutics of faith and a
   hermeneutics of suspicion. This was the dilemma that faced
   the Romantics of the early nineteenth century, to whom we
   turn in our next chapter.

Activities and Questions

1. What are the main strengths and weaknesses of the
   hermeneutics of Thomas Aquinas?

2. We tend to be very suspicious of *eisegesis*, often arguing that
   if something is not there in the text, we have no right to
   impose it on it. But it could be said that *all* reading has an element of eisegesis in it. In what way, or ways, is this true?

3. Erasmus was notoriously opposed to the dogmas of the
   church, and in his famous work *The Praise of Folly* he even
   attacks the slipperiness of "theologians," seemingly even
   including Paul. Read the following excerpt from this work
   carefully and consider the questions about Scripture and theological interpretation to which it gives rise. Who, or what,
   then, are we to trust? Erasmus complains of when "theologians are allowed to stretch heaven, that is, the Scriptures, as
   a sheepskin. If we can give credence to Jerome, who knew five
   languages, there are some contradictory words in Paul. When
   he spoke to the Athenians, he twisted what he read on the
   altar into an argument for the Christian faith, omitting what
   was not for his purpose, and selecting only two from the end,
   'to the Unknown God.' The actual inscription reads, 'To the
   Gods of Asia, Europe and Africa, and to the Unknown Gods,

and the Gods of Strangers.' I feel that the sons of theologians follow his example today, when they accommodate for their own purposes four or five words out of context, or even change in meaning . . . there is no limit to their false exegesis. He [an unnamed theologian] has squeezed from Luke words so opposed to the spirit of Christ as fire is to water." (Quoted in *The Essential Erasmus*)

4. What are the characteristics of Luther and Calvin in their hermeneutical thinking that you would describe as "modern"? How do they change the very character of *theology* from that of the Middle Ages?

5. Is it still necessary to opt for *either* a sacred *or* a secular hermeneutic? Do we have to lead two lives, or is it possible in our time to reunite sacred and secular reading? Do you think it is possible to validate by proper hermeneutics the authority of the Bible, as opposed to any other text, after the Age of Reason?

Chapter Four

Friedrich Schleiermacher and the Age of Romanticism

1 The Bible and History

As we move nearer to the nineteenth century we find everywhere a biblical criticism and a hermeneutics that are firmly established on "Enlightenment" principles, that is, on the use of reason in what philosophy would call an "empirical" manner of reading and interpretation and what the English writer Anthony Collins (1676–1729) refers to as "the common rules of grammar and logic." The Bible now comes under the glare of a self-conscious critical scrutiny, often regarded more as an interesting work from antiquity than as a sacred text. In 1724, Collins published his book entitled *Discourse of the Grounds and Reasons of the Christian Religion*, having previously published in 1707 his *Essay Concerning the Use of Reason*. Collins's work is important, since he argued that early Christianity was essentially a literary adaptation of the earlier narratives and texts of the Hebrew Bible. In other words, Christianity very largely sprang out of a particular way of *reading* the Old Testament as types, allegories, and prophecies of the future events and persons of the New Testament. An exercise in literary history was now presuming to answer questions about the origin and nature of Christianity itself. (This, as we have seen, has some truth in it, although there is more to the story than that. For some people, however, this may be a debatable point.)

69

Collins was a freethinker—a new kind of hermeneut quite unlike all those whom we have studied so far, even Chladenius, who was, as you will recall, anxious to protect the Bible from the corrosive effects of his otherwise rational theories. But for Collins, the Bible must take its chance alongside every other text. In the eighteenth century, hermeneutics and the interpretation of the Bible finally moved largely away from the church and readers whose purpose was pious or religious, to find its focus in the academy and university and in readers whose purpose was essentially academic.

It was during this century in England and Germany that the business of reading the Bible became both a learned and *skeptical* exercise. Edward Gibbon's (1737–94) great work, *The History of the Decline and Fall of the Roman Empire* (1776–88), set a new standard for historical inquiry and its march forward that set little or no store by the effective claims of faith or religious belief.

A little earlier (although his famous *Fragments* were published only posthumously by G. E. Lessing in 1774–78), the German H. S. Reimarus (1694–1768), who was professor of Oriental languages in a Hamburg *Gymnasium*, sought to recover the lost "historical Jesus" by his reading of the Gospels as early Christian elaborations on the simple "facts" by speculation and mythologizing. The Bible was to be read as Oriental stories through which, by the tools of reason, philology, and the apparatus of modern learning a portrait of the true Jesus might be recovered. Reimarus was the great iconoclast (or "breaker of idols") who is sometimes credited with being the first in the line of scholars who have embarked on the "quest for the historical Jesus," but it should be clear that his purpose was explicitly antitheological and anti-Christian. For Reimarus the cold light of history evacuates religious belief, and his aim was to show that the real Jesus of Nazareth, once recovered, could not be the basis for Christian faith. More will be said shortly about this growth of *historical criticism* in the development of hermeneutics.

(Hermeneutics and theology, as must be abundantly obvious by now, are never far apart. Reimarus was actually exploiting the potential split between the Jesus of *history* and the Christ of *faith* evident in the rather anxious remark of the reformer Philipp Melanchthon (1497–1560) when he said, "Unless one knows why Christ took upon himself human flesh and was crucified, what advantage would accrue from having learned his life's history?" Reimarus simply turns this around. If for Melanchthon the Christ of faith precedes and enlightens for us the Jesus of history, for Reimarus the Jesus of history, once recovered by a particular reading of the Bible, would obliterate the Christ of faith.)

Another important figure that demands mention is Robert Lowth (1710–87), bishop of London. Like Anthony Collins, Lowth was interested in the literature of the Hebrew Bible, though he was far more learned than Collins and an excellent Hebraist. In 1753, Lowth published (in Latin) his Oxford lectures *On the Sacred Poetry of the Hebrews*. An Anglican clergyman, Lowth had also been an academic and as a relatively young man was elected as professor of poetry at the University of Oxford. (Until the nineteenth century, all the lectures of the professor of poetry were required to be delivered in Latin!) The combination of Hebrew scholar and poet in Lowth is interesting and not without importance for us. Lowth, quite literally, rediscovered the form and structure of Hebrew poetry, quite different from classical or modern poetic models, which are based largely on principles of rhythm and rhyme. Hebrew verse, Lowth claimed, was based on the principle of *parallelism*, lines that appear to repeat or almost repeat one another in a variety of subtle ways. Here are two examples of what I mean. The first is familiar enough. It is the victory song of the women of Israel in 1 Samuel 18:7.

> Saul has killed his thousands,
> and David his ten thousands.

If Saul's reaction to this comparison of their achievements is anything to go by, it is a good example of the power of poetry! The second is from Psalm 69:2.

I sink in deep mire,
where there is no foothold;
I have come into deep waters,
and the flood sweeps over me.

Is the psalmist simply repeating himself? Or, rather, does not the second line add dramatically to the first in a kind of incremental progression?

Although the technical details of Lowth's "discovery" are not particularly our concern here, it is important to realize that this is a major step forward in the understanding of the Bible *as literature*. Lowth is reading these texts in the first instance as literary masterpieces, and from this draws his conclusions. He speaks of the "writings of Moses" as some of the earliest examples of poetry, and to these he adds (from Genesis) the "inspired benedictions" of Isaac and Jacob. For the Hebrews, he affirmed, poetry stood preeminent as "the highest commendation of science and erudition." (Reimarus, in short, is studying the Bible as *history*; Lowth is studying it as *literature*—meanwhile, *theology* is now having to take its chance!)

> Reimarus, in short, is studying the Bible as *history*; Lowth is studying it as *literature*—meanwhile, *theology* is now having to take its chance!

It might not be an overestimation to say that Lowth's lectures *On the Sacred Poetry of the Hebrews*, which were translated into German long before they were translated into English, transformed the manner in which we read and interpret the poetic parts of the Bible, and were a herald of the movement of mind and spirit in Germany, England, and France called *romanticism*. This movement constituted a crucial shift in hermeneutical theory and understanding, and we are still assessing the consequences of it today.

Lowth's Lecture 17 is entitled "Of the Sublime of Passion." He emphasizes the importance of the "language of poetry" in the exercise of the imagination and for "exciting the passions." Yet, drawing directly on the writings of Aristotle in the *Poetics*, Lowth insists that the reading of poetry should not inflame the passions, thus making them unruly, but rather, he said, "it is the office of poetry to incite, to direct, to temper the passions, and not to extinguish them." Taking Aristotle as our guide, this is as true of the poetry of the Bible as of any other poetry. (Imagine the horror Luther would have felt at this critical move from a "pagan" writer!) As regards the Hebrew texts of the Old Testament, this poetic activity is linked directly to liturgical practice in worship, and is a means of understanding more clearly how the ancient Jews sang the praises of God. Again, we see how literary insights are now feeding theological conclusions. Here is the opening paragraph of Lowth's nineteenth lecture, where we notice how he brings in the art of music and performance as well as poetry.

> The origin and earliest application of the Hebrew poetry have, I think, been clearly traced into the service of religion. To celebrate in hymns and songs the praises of Almighty God; to decorate the worship of the Most High with all the charms and graces of harmony; to give force and energy to the devout affections was the sublime employment of the Sacred Muse. It is more than probable, that the very early use of sacred music in the public worship of the Hebrews, contributed not a little to the peculiar character of their poetry, and might impart to it that appropriate form, which, though chiefly adapted to this particular purpose, it nevertheless preserves on every other occasion. But in order to explain this matter more clearly, it will be necessary to premise a few observations concerning the ancient Hebrew mode of chanting their sacred hymns. (Lowth, quoted in John Drury, ed., *Critics of the Bible, 1724–1873*)

Now, how does all this help us in our study of hermeneutics? Well, first, note how Lowth's concerns in reading the Bible are still essentially historical. For him as for others in the eighteenth and nineteenth centuries, to read was to reach back to the historical origins and conditions that were hidden within the text. These were to be brought to light by proper processes of interpretation, rather as an excavation in archaeology digs up its truths from the earth where they lie hidden and overlaid by the centuries. The biblical interpreter must carefully scrape away the layers of dirt and the additions of later cultures onto the text in order to recover the truth beneath in its pristine splendor. Second, Lowth looks forward to romanticism in his recovery (via Aristotle) of the sublime and emotive power of poetic texts such as, for instance, the psalms. Reading is a matter of feeling and the stimulation of the emotions, and by reason of Lowth's "discovery" we can now once again read and even sing these psalms with something of the response and feelings of the ancient Hebrews themselves! Reading the Bible has finally moved beyond the walls of the church and its theological debates, and yet, at the same time, for Lowth (though certainly not for Reimarus) his work calls on the theologians to respond, if they will. Still, the underlying implications are clear. Lowth is setting a new agenda for reading, and in this new age of critical hermeneutics a crucial question is asked: What is the nature of the Bible's *authority*, and is it in the end different from the authority of any other literary or historical text?

2   Johann Salomo Semler (1725–91) and the Canon of Scripture

Johann Salomo Semler (1725–91) was professor of theology at the University of Halle in Germany. Still writing within the Lutheran tradition, Semler gave extensive consideration to the theory of hermeneutics and its bearing on our reception of the Bible. In a work on theological hermeneutics published in 1760, Semler wrote:

> The most important thing, in short, in hermeneutical skill depends upon one's knowing the Bible's use of language properly and precisely, as well as distinguishing and representing to oneself the historical circumstances of a biblical discourse; and on one's being able to speak today of these matters in such a way as the changed times and circumstances of our fellow-men demand. . . . All the rest of hermeneutics can be reduced to these two things. (Semler, quoted in Frei, *The Eclipse of Biblical Narrative*)

This is a pretty categorical statement, and with scholars like Semler hermeneutics has moved finally and without reserve into the university and its classrooms. In this passage you can see the learned professor speaking to his students and requiring of them the willing suspension of religious belief and the acquiring of particular skills as they get down to their critical task. This is a business requiring precise linguistic knowledge and learning and a clear sense of *cultural relativity*—we need to be acutely aware of our *own* cultural circumstances, as well as our cultural differences from those of the ancient biblical texts.

One of the major consequences of Semler's labors was the fragmentation of the unity of the Bible and the breakup of the traditional unity of the *canon*. How so? We have seen in chapter 2 how the canon of the Christian Bible developed over the first few centuries of the church and became the yardstick of authority, reaffirmed confidently by Luther's principle of *sola scriptura*. The canon of Scripture had been for almost two millennia the collection of authorized texts against which the Christian tradition was measured and maintained. To remind ourselves briefly, from the earliest days of the church it was important to establish which texts were canonical and authoritative (e.g., the four Gospels), and which were not (e.g., the apocryphal Gospel of Thomas). Although the canon was never completely stable (Luther, for example, thought that the book of Revelation should be left out), nevertheless its establishment ensured both the broad *unity* of Scripture and its *authority* as a comprehensive collection of texts. (In modern scholarship, C. F. D. Moule in his book *The Birth of the New Testament* argues that in spite of the contradictions and differences between its books, the New Testament does reflect a remarkable unity, implying that the hand of God was at work in their selection. His argument is not unpersuasive.)

But to take a more lighthearted diversion for a moment, in his book *The Tabloid Bible* (1998) Nick Page makes some serious points while presenting biblical incidents in the manner of the *Sun* or *Mirror* tabloid newspapers. His "reporter" comments on Paul:

Paul has become famous for his letters to churches throughout Asia Minor. Many churches are now basing their understanding of the Christian faith on Paul's "epistles," as they are
known.

"I"m just trying to make sense of everything that happened," said Paul. *"Obviously not all my letters are equally
important.* There are several to Aunty Beryl that are merely
thanking her for my birthday present." (Page, *Tabloid Bible*;
emphasis added)

The point is that in Semler's hermeneutics not all books of the
Bible are of equal importance and historical reliability. Some are
more authentic and useful than others. In a major work on the
canon, published between 1771 and 1775, Semler held in question "the formerly commonly held assertions of the general and
undifferentiated divinity of the whole so-called Bible." The discerning (and learned) reader must discriminate, by proper academic criteria, between texts that are "reliable" and those that are
less so, and learn, says Semler, "to judge for himself."

What we have here is a serious and direct threat to "so-called"
sacred Scripture and its unity and authority. The science of
hermeneutics is here opposing itself to the whole tradition, which
understands the Bible, and *all* the Bible taken together, as the
Word of God. Critical reading itself, in short, has become a threat
to biblical authority.

Another learned German academic, Johann Gottfried Eichhorn (1752–1827), a professor of philosophy, wrote massive scholarly "Introductions" to both the Old and the New Testaments.
Eichhorn summarily dismissed much of the Old Testament as
merely primitive outpourings of an almost prehistoric and unsophisticated people (unsophisticated, that is, as compared to civilization defined in terms of German Enlightenment scholarship),
and he proposed that the truth and validity of Christian claims
could only be laboriously picked out and extracted from the primitive ramblings of a people who lacked the necessary philosophical and linguistic skills that "modern" theology has developed and
required. Through hermeneutics, not only the Bible but religion

itself was becoming a scholarly business.

It is hardly surprising that, at the same time in the eighteenth and early nineteenth centuries, evangelical and pietist movements in England and Germany were turning their backs on such abstruse scholarship, and resorting to a variety of kinds of fundamentalist readings of the Bible that simply claimed every word was literally true. This kind of reading the English poet and thinker Samuel Taylor Coleridge summarily dismissed as "bibliolatry"— the mindless reading of the text as itself, in effect, divine. The gap between the hermeneutics of faith and the hermeneutics of suspicion seemed absolute and unbridgeable.

3   Immanuel Kant (1724–1804) and the Romantic Spirit

We are not engaged in an exercise in philosophy or philosophical theology, but rather in a survey on how texts, and especially biblical texts, are read and understood. At the same time we have to recognize that such exercises cannot ultimately be separated from one another. Hermeneutics is no optional extra. And so we cannot proceed farther into the age of romanticism and the nineteenth century without a very brief acknowledgment of the crucial work of the German philosopher Immanuel Kant (1724–1804), who, quite literally, changed the way in which people in the West thought, and thought of themselves. Kant's thinking and writings are vast and complex, and we need to acknowledge that they amount to a very great deal more than is suggested here. Two points will suffice for our purposes.

Kant begins a famous essay entitled "An Answer to the Question 'What Is Enlightenment?'" written in 1784, with these words:

> *Enlightenment is man's emergence from his self-incurred immaturity. Immaturity* is the inability to use one's understanding without the guidance of another. This immaturity is *self-incurred* if its cause is not lack of understanding, but lack of resolution and courage to use it without the guidance of another. The motto of enlightenment is therefore: *Sapere*

aude! Have courage to use your *own* understanding! (Kant, in Reiss, ed. *Political Writings*)

By now we should be familiar with this kind of attitude. Kant follows Descartes in his emphasis on thinking, and Eichhorn and others in his sense that modern humankind is entering into a new maturity before unknown. Elsewhere, in a book entitled *Religion within the Limits of Reason Alone* (1793), Kant "demythologizes" Western religion and attempts to demonstrate that its long history is merely a projection of our moral sensibilities. In short, we should now be growing out of such childish things.

For the reader of texts—to keep to our specific concerns—Kant means that you should not rely on the *authority* of others, whether it is the church or the professor. Read for yourself. You, yes, *you* can understand this or any text as well as I can (provided you have equipped yourself with the necessary *skills* of language, philology, and so on).

Second, and more broadly, Kant questioned the objectivity of the world "out there." He was not suggesting that it does not exist, but rather that it is only possible to perceive and understand it on our own terms, and not absolutely. In a famous phrase from romanticism, "we half create what we perceive." In other words, as we have already seen in chapter 1, the differences between us mean that we see the world in different ways—what for me is sublime, for you is simply terrifying. What I think is beautiful, you may see as ugly. Thus the reader does not contemplate a text in which there is "a meaning," but brings to the text (and to the world) his or her own perspectives and even prejudices. We may, indeed, misunderstand a text (through ignorance or pigheadedness), but often we just have different understandings, one not necessarily any better or worse than another. The end result of this suggestion is the famous question asked of one professor of literature, "Is there a text in the class, or is it just us?" (The professor in question is called Stanley Fish, and we shall come back to him in chapter 6.)

Furthermore, for Kant, interpretation and indeed thinking itself are not merely exercises of the reason, but must also involve intuitions and the realm of the *imagination*. As the English poet William Blake put it in his poem *The Everlasting Gospel* (ca. 1818):

Both read the Bible day and night,
But thou read'st black where I read white.

For the romantic poets and thinkers of the early nineteenth century—especially in England and Germany, such as Coleridge, Wordsworth, Goethe, and Hölderlin—after first the age of reason and then after Kant, the major problem was how to read the Bible and be true to the *critical* demands of scholars like Semler, yet also to read it in the light of the new romantic poetry with its emphasis on the supernatural and the claims of *feelings and emotions*. In their time the church and its authority was, it seemed, disintegrating, as was the authority of the Bible, and what they began to seek was a new *mythology*—a new worldview in the context of which they could read and understand. What was happening was what is now known as a *paradigm shift* in understanding such as took place when the Renaissance and the Reformation replaced the worldview of the Middle Ages. In short, people were seeking a new way of describing the world. (Another huge paradigm shift in scientific thinking nearer our own times was the "discovery" of relativity that replaced a Newtonian worldview with that of Albert Einstein. It, too, has had an enormous effect on how we read and understand texts. We shall come back to this in more detail a little later, in chapter 5.)

Myth, as we shall see later on, became a crucial word in the nineteenth century. Looking back to particular events in *history*—such as the life of Jesus—the great romantic hermeneuts also sought to read the Bible as a text of *timeless* truths, true for all times and places. (Reimarus, you will recall, sought to undermine the claims of Christianity by trying to locate the specific *historical* Jesus.)

But how was the Bible to become, again, relevant, let alone true for their time? For another characteristic of the romantic spirit, as it perceived the changing of the sociopolitical world order after the French Revolution and the decay of the so-called *ancien régime*, was the sense of breakup and *fragmentation*. The Bible itself (and by extension all texts), once read as a seamless unity, was now read as fragments or a series of fragments from which, at best, we can be afforded gleams and slivers of truth and glory. Reading became as much a case of filling in the gaps and seeing what is not there in the text as it was a matter of reading what *is* on the page. The romantics, as they lamented what they saw as the breaking down of the ancient order of things, regarded the old texts as, at best, broken remembrances of things past and read them as a *reconstruction* of half-forgotten truths. Their obsession with ruins, and especially ruined medieval abbeys like Fountains or Rievaulx in Yorkshire, extended to the Bible as a beautiful and still valuable but essentially ruined memorial of a world past and gone. The poet William Wordsworth expressed this sense of loss in his poem "Intimations of Immortality":

> Whither is fled the visionary gleam?
> Where is it now, the glory and the dream?

For many of the romantics, the Bible now simply took its place alongside the rest of literature, merely one element in what Goethe termed *Weltliteratur* ("world literature"). No longer was there a separate hermeneutic for reading the Bible, as there was even for Chladenius, but the Bible was to be read like any other book and left to take its chances—although, as we shall see in a moment, in Coleridge and Schleiermacher, it was never quite that simple. Nevertheless, for the first time in the history we have been following, reading became an activity guided not by *belief* in a tradition, God, and theology, but actually by *unbelief* and atheism. The age of reason and the shifting of the political map of Europe had done their work. Thus for the poet Shelley, Jesus was simply a fellow poet and a hero alongside others from mythology and history. For the atheist Shelley, the Bible is read as poetry alongside such myths as that of Prometheus, who stole fire from the gods for the benefit of humans and was punished accordingly, yet becomes a hero figure celebrated in romantic verse. Shelley ends his epic poem *Prometheus Unbound* (1820) with these magnificent words, not lamenting fragmentation but celebrating the freedom of heroism:

> This, like thy glory, Titan, is to be
> Good, great and joyous, beautiful and free;
> *This is alone Life, Joy, Empire, and Victory.* [Emphasis added]

4 Samuel Taylor Coleridge, *Confessions of an Inquiring Spirit*, 1840

That, however, is by no means the end of the story for biblical hermeneutics. The English romantic poet, philosopher, and theologian Samuel Taylor Coleridge (1772–1834) was the son of an Anglican clergyman who anticipated many others in the nineteenth century by combining a restless, skeptical mind and a dislike of the theological and spiritual claims of the church with an equally profound sense of the holiness of Scripture. A voracious reader and an excellent linguist, Coleridge was fascinated by language and what happens in the process of reading. Indeed, his *Biographia Literaria* (1817), or "Literary Life," is in some ways an exercise in encouraging its reader to become self-reflective *in the very act of reading*. The book may be said to be not so much a source of information about his life, poetry, and philosophy as an incentive to ponder on how meaning is generated in the mind of the reader. Coleridge wants us to think about ourselves as we read and struggle to make sense of his admittedly often difficult text. He will, for example, take you through a complex philosophical argument and then pause with a question, the point being not so much that we solve its mystery, but that we come to understand a little more how we actually think through and understand it with all its difficulties.

Coleridge's collection of "letters" entitled *Confessions of an Inquiring Spirit* was published posthumously, edited by his nephew Henry Nelson Coleridge with the following "Advertisement." It is worth quoting in full.

The following Letters on the Inspiration of the Scriptures were left by Mr. Coleridge in Ms. at his death. The Reader will find in them a key to most of the Biblical criticism scattered throughout the Author's own writings, and an affectionate, pious, and, as the Editor humbly believes, a profoundly wise attempt to place the study of the Written Word on its only sure foundation,—a deep sense of God's holiness and truth, and a consequent reverence for that Light—the image of Himself—which He has kindled in every one of His rational creatures. (Coleridge, *Confessions of an Inquiring Spirit.*)

Note here the emphasis on *rationality*—Coleridge is, after all, still a child of the eighteenth century. At the same time, the reading of the written Word is based on a prior *feeling* which Coleridge identifies as a sense of the holiness and truth of God. For him, biblical interpretation is a proper meeting of the irrational and the rational—it is a hermeneutics of faith *and* a hermeneutics of suspicion at one and the same time. He admits that reading begins with a felt need born of his own awareness of inadequacy and limit. As a reader he comes to the text, he readily admits, as one "who is neither fair nor saintly, but who—groaning under a deep sense of infirmity and manifold imperfection—feels the want, the necessity, of religious support." In other words, Coleridge comes to the Bible not so much seeking to understand, or with a mind soothed by sanctity, but rather to find consolation for his wounded soul.

For Coleridge this in no way implies any kind of hermeneutical fundamentalism. The solution to his initial sense of unworthiness and imperfection does not lie *in* the biblical text like a hidden meaning to be excavated by interpretive procedures. Rather, reading for Coleridge is an interactive business between reader and text, which initiates a kind of voyage of discovery. Here is a key passage in his *Confessions* from the beginning of Letter II:

In my last letter I said that . . . in the Bible there is more that *finds* me than I have experienced in all other books together; . . . the words of the Bible find me at greater depths of my

being; and that whatever finds me brings with it an irre-
sistible evidence of its having proceeded from the Holy
Spirit. (Coleridge, *Confessions of an Inquiring Spirit*)

Coleridge is a religious, but at the same time a highly intelligent, reader of the Bible. He hates what he calls "bibliolatry"—
that is, the unthinking assumption that the truth is simply there
in the text, clear and without contradiction, or to be found without interpretive labor. Like others after him in the nineteenth century, he encouraged us to read the Bible critically *like any other book*
and then, but only then, might we discover its uniqueness. Reading is an adventure of discovery and, above all, self-discovery.

Furthermore, true to the principle of the hermeneutic circle,
he insisted that you have to read the Bible *as a whole*, in all its various, difficult, and sometimes contradictory parts, in order to discover what it is about. You should not pick and choose, and the
honest reader must not eliminate those bits which he or she finds
difficult or even offensive, such as the notorious last verse of Psalm
137:

Happy shall they be who take your little ones
and dash them against the rock!

However unpalatable we may find this, it is in the written Word
too! And we read it, just as we must read *all* of Shakespeare, the
great and the not so great, the well known and the little known, if
we are to understand him. I use this example because, in the *Confessions*, Coleridge places his beloved Shakespeare alongside the
Bible as another great instance of literature—the same in genius,
yet somehow different. And the difference between Shakespeare
and the Bible can be found only *through reading*.

5   Friedrich Schleiermacher (1768–1834) and the Handwritten Manuscripts

Friedrich Schleiermacher was born of German pietist stock, and at
the same time was a formidably learned theologian and philosopher,

the author of some of the most abstract and systematic works of Christian theology ever written. Writing after Kant, he gave much reflection to questions of *epistemology*—that is, thinking about the nature of knowledge and how we think and come to know. At the same time, Schleiermacher remained something of a pietist, a devout man who still said his prayers humbly. These two elements, piety and a fierce intellectualism, remain central to his hermeneutics.

Schleiermacher never published a formal work on hermeneutics—all we have are the "handwritten manuscripts" of his lecture notes for students. Nevertheless, hermeneutical reflection lies at the very heart of all his concerns. The theologian must also be the reflective hermeneut, always thinking about the processes of reading. We can here only scratch the surface of these reflections, but their importance cannot be overestimated for the story to be told in the remainder of this book. Schleiermacher is the first, and perhaps the greatest, of modern hermeneuts.

First, he insisted that reading is an *art* and that the reader of a text must be as much an artist as its author. In a sense, reading is as creative as the act of writing itself. The negotiations that go on between text and reader are born out of two anxieties: the first is the anxiety to be understood (which is why we write), and the second is the anxiety to understand (which is why we read). In order to combat this second anxiety, the reader must be thoroughly disciplined and "artistically sound." But this does not mean, Schleiermacher insists, that such a reader ever comes to rest in final conclusions that mark the end and conclusion of the reading process. On the contrary, "the hermeneutical task moves constantly," and each interpretation only prompts further insights and new "conversations," rather as when we are climbing a mountain and we think we have reached the summit only to realize that there are other, higher summits beyond, hidden by the little rise over which we have momentarily triumphed. The final summit of hermeneutics is forever lost in the clouds.

Schleiermacher insists that hermeneutical principles must be universal, and neither the Bible nor the theologian is granted any special privileges. If they are to have validity, they must be equally applicable to all texts without exception. Under this universal rule, *all* interpretation is divided into two parts:

(1) *psychological* interpretation, which is concerned with the interplay between the reader and the text;
(2) *grammatical* interpretation, which requires knowledge and the careful examination of the linguistic and syntactical structures of the text and its language.

The interpreter moves constantly between these two poles, the one always checking the other. Any judgments we may make or conclusions we may reach must be tested against the almost scientific demands of grammatical interpretation. In other words, our personal response is important, but it must never be *just* personal. We must test it against the linguistic demands of the text itself.

There may be varying degrees of *significance* in a text. In this sense, not all texts are equal. Generally where the language and theme are commonplace, a text will be minimally significant. But where thought and language are extraordinary and complex, Schleiermacher believes we may expect maximum significance.

Schleiermacher is a careful, almost scientific reader, yet he never forgets his pietist background and its reverent attitude toward the Bible. Two important points must finally be noted in this very brief survey of his main hermeneutical principles.

First, in a famous sentence, Schleiermacher insisted that it is the interpreter's task "to understand the text at first as well as and then even better than its author." At first sight this might seem rather puzzling, but actually it makes perfectly good sense if you stop and think about it. For example, I may read an essay that you have written and say to you, "Do you realize what you have said here?" You, having read the passage again may, perhaps, admit that I am right and you had not quite appreciated what you were saying. Thus it might be the case that, with the benefit of scholarly research, the distance of history, and the ability to stand back from his social and cultural milieu, we may be able to claim to understand Paul's epistles *even better than he understood them himself.*

That is, if we are careful hermeneuts! We may know things of which he was unaware, being too close to them.

Second, Schleiermacher quite explicitly expounds the principle of our old friend the hermeneutic circle, seen in terms of the continual interplay between the particular parts of the text and its complete whole. Reading a part, we begin to build up a picture of the whole, and this overall picture we test by returning again to the claims of the specific and particular elements in the writing.

Summary

We might summarize the main points of this chapter as follows:

1. The broad shift in the eighteenth century away from a hermeneutics of faith and toward a hermeneutics of suspicion based on the exercise of human reason.
2. The development of a modern sense of "history" and its disintegrative impact on the unity of the biblical canon and the authority of Scripture.
3. Robert Lowth's "rediscovery" of Hebrew poetics.
4. Kant's idealist philosophy and the acknowledgment of the creative mind of the reader.
5. Coleridge's exploration in *Confessions of an Inquiring Spirit* of how the Bible "finds him" in the depths of his being, and the rejection of "bibliolatry."
6. Friedrich Schleiermacher, the father of modern hermeneutics, and the development of hermeneutics as a science.

Activities and Questions

1. Find examples of parallelism in the Hebrew Bible and analyze the way in which each one works. Try to ascertain the *differences* between various kinds of parallelism.
2. Semler and Eichhorn thought that they were marching on the high road of progress and civilization away from the primitive, though still necessary, "beginnings" of religion in the

biblical texts, into the clearer light of modern culture and learning.

As *you* read the Bible today, how far do you think that their attitude is valid? Would it be possible to think like this now? If not, why not?

If we think that *we* are superior to these Enlightenment critics of the eighteenth century, are we not falling into the same trap as they did if we imagine that the twenty-first century is more "enlightened" than they were?

3. Do you think that it is possible to read the Bible "like any other book"? Think very carefully about this. The Bible is a collection of texts written in human languages. Why should it be *intrinsically* different from the writings of, say, Shakespeare or Dante?

4. Do you think that the hermeneutics that have been outlined in this chapter represent progress or regression in the art of reading the Bible? Think carefully about the *criteria* you are using to make a response to this question.

5. Take a familiar passage from the letters of Paul, say 1 Corinthians 13, the great "hymn to love," and read it very carefully in a modern translation. In what sense might we claim to understand this passage even better than its author did? Why do you think that Schleiermacher is so insistent on this principle in his hermeneutics?

Chapter Five

The Nineteenth Century

1 The Critical Spirit and the Will to Believe

If the eighteenth century was the age of reason, then we might call the nineteenth century the age of science. But what, you might ask, has this statement got to do with our subject of hermeneutics? The answer is, a great deal. When, in 1859, Charles Darwin published his famous work *On the Origin of Species*, science seemed to throw down the gauntlet to the truth and accuracy of the Bible narratives. Although Darwin's thesis about evolution was not exactly new, he was the first person to present it in the context of a carefully and scientifically researched narrative. If the biblical accounts of the creation in the book of Genesis, for example, could no longer be accepted as true *scientifically*, in what sense were they true at all? Had science disproved their truth, and in what sense were they valid at all? Were they just *myths*, and what was the status of "myth"? (The Greek word from which "myth" is derived meant "story," and later came to mean something like a legendary tale or fable. Look up 1 Timothy 1:4; 2 Timothy 4:4; and above all 1 Timothy 4:7, which speak of "profane myths and old wives tales.")

Darwin himself, though he had once been destined for the priesthood, was an agnostic. But even more troubling, professed Christians like Bishop Colenso of Natal were challenging the traditionally understood divine origins and historical accuracy of the

Bible. Bishop Colenso published his notorious book *The Penta-teuch and the Book of Joshua Critically Examined* between 1862 and 1879, and was promptly deposed from his diocese by his senior bishop, Bishop Gray of Cape Town. The Bible was not even safe from bishops!

For many in the nineteenth century the critical reading of the Bible on scientific principles posed enormous problems for belief, and yet the will to believe in its truth remained powerful. Such readers seemed to be caught between the ancient world of faith and the modern age of suspicion, a state graphically described by Matthew Arnold in his poem "Stanzas from the Grande Char-treuse" (1855) as

> Wandering between two worlds, one dead,
> The other powerless to be born.

The modern reader of the Bible seemed to be truly homeless. Arnold himself proposed a solution by reading the Bible purely as *poetry*, thereby avoiding the rigorous, critical demands of science. In an essay entitled "The Study of Poetry," he suggested that "more and more mankind will discover that we have to turn to poetry to interpret life for us, to console us, to sustain us" and "sci-ence . . . will appear incomplete without it." We might go farther and say that not only will we not be able to do without poetry, but it will be a kind of interpreter for us as we read the Bible. Thus, as we encounter in Paul's letters terms like "grace" or "justifica-tion," we should understand them as *poetic symbols*, avoiding the "science" of theology altogether.

> Terms, in short, which with Paul are *literary* terms, theolo-gians have employed as if they were *scientific* terms. (Matthew Arnold, *Literature and Dogma*, 1873)

Reading the Bible, then, was separated by Arnold from the business of theology altogether—a concept that would have been altogether foreign to both Aquinas and Luther. We shall return later, in chapter 7, to the idea of reading the bible as literature.

2 David Friedrich Strauss, *Das Leben Jesu* (1835)

Like Schleiermacher, David Friedrich Strauss (1808–74) was a German intellectual, a philosopher and theologian. A student of the philosopher Hegel, his greatest work was his massive *Life of Jesus*, which is possibly the single most important book in the whole history of nineteenth-century hermeneutics. Strauss's work is a hermeneutics of suspicion with a vengeance! His approach to biblical interpretation, with its origins in Hegelian philosophy, was based on scientific method, and is an example of what was later to be called *German Higher Criticism*, that is, "the critical study of the literary methods and sources used by the [biblical] authors"(*Oxford Dictionary of the Christian Church*, 3d ed.). Strauss wished to free the reading of Scripture entirely from all religious and dogmatic presuppositions, and began his study of the Gospels from two clear principles:

1. Miracles do not happen, but that people may believe in them is the result of demonstrable facts of human nature.
2. All ancient history, sacred *or* profane, is to be treated alike. The Bible is to be given no special privileges.

Reading the Gospels, Strauss asserts that "here we stand upon purely mythical-poetical ground." But, unlike Matthew Arnold, he does not hold much store by poetry, regarding it as something rather primitive, to be seen through by the bright light of modern scientific research. The task of the hermeneut is to unravel this primitive *myth* and to discover the truth, which is accessible only by rigorous scientific inquiry. His process is close to what the twentieth-century German scholar Rudolf Bultmann was to call *demythologizing*, a term to which we shall return in chapter 6.

Strauss shows an impatience with the Christian history of hermeneutics of faith, and in particular what he calls the "tedious centuries of the Middle Ages," and sees his task as "to translate the language of a former age into that of today." Only then will true clarity be achieved. For him the events described in the Gospels, all the miracles and even the resurrection itself, are ultimately attributable to natural causes, and the careful reader must search for the truth to be discovered hidden beneath their miraculous coverings. In many ways, Strauss was not so very far from the earlier work of Reimarus and Eichhorn and their belief in the fundamentally primitive and mythic nature of the biblical texts. Modern scholarship suggests that the Gospels were written long after the "events" of Jesus' life, and that they are themselves interpretations of those events, wrapping up experiences and states of feeling in the imaginative symbols of their day. The interpreter of the Bible is, therefore, interpreting interpretations, stripping away layers of mythical accretions with modern tools of philology, philosophy, and science. Like Reimarus in the eighteenth century, Strauss effectively suggests that the faith of the church was not based on anything like the "real" Jesus who lies hidden behind the Gospel narratives.

Careful reading of the Gospels, for Strauss, must undercut religion and its assumptions. But if Christianity is thus destroyed *critically*, it may be rediscovered as legitimated in the reflections of modern philosophy. His hermeneutics seeks a Christianity suited to the modern age and distinct from its historical origins and traditions in Scripture. It is a radical hermeneutics, and it is not insignificant for English readers that one of Strauss's earliest disciples was the novelist George Eliot, who as a young woman translated his *Leben Jesu* into English as *The Life of Jesus Critically Examined* (1846) before finally abandoning her own Christian faith for a "religion of humanity," which she explored in such great novels as *Adam Bede* (1859) and *Middlemarch* (1871–72). Through Strauss the Bible had indeed joined the ranks of imaginative, even fictional, literature through a universal hermeneutic that seemed to have destroyed its sacred status once and for all.

3   The Quest for the Historical Jesus

Eighteenth-century hermeneutics, we might say, more or less invented the modern understanding of *history*, and by the nineteenth century the hermeneut's task had become effectively a branch of philosophy, so that, with scholars like Strauss, the historical origins of the biblical texts were almost lost sight of.

According to the great historian Leopold von Ranke (1795–1886), the historian's task was to know the literal events, or "how it actually happened," and the Gospels as texts resting on purely mythical-poetical ground gave us no direct clue to the actual historical Jesus. Jesus, it seemed, had vanished from sight in the mists of philosophical speculation.

Biblical critics in Germany actually distinguished between two understandings of the term "history," described in the German words *Historie* and *Geschichte*. *Historie* is a description of how events actually happened; *Geschichte* is a description of what events *mean*, both to those who first experienced them and to us now. In other words, *Geschichte* is also concerned with contemporary present-day experience. History is not just about the past; it is also about the present. (In one way or another, "historical-critical" methods have continued to dominate the academic study of the Bible up to the present day.)

> In one way or another, "historical-critical" methods have continued to dominate the academic study of the Bible up to the present day.

How, then, do we read the Gospels "as history," or as descriptions of events that happened? Joseph-Ernest Renan (1823–92) was a French orientalist who visited the Holy Land and is best known for his book *La Vie de Jésus* [*The Life of Jesus*] (1863). His romantic reading of the New Testament places its world firmly within the blue haze of the nineteenth-century imagination, a hermeneutics set not in the first century C.E. but firmly in the mind of the modern reader. Albert Schweitzer describes Renan's work in his own great book, *The Quest of the Historical Jesus* (1906):

> He offered his readers a Jesus who was alive, whom he, with his artistic imagination, had met under the blue heaven of Galilee, and whose features his inspired pencil has seized. People's attention was arrested, and they thought they could see Jesus, because Renan had the skill to make them see blue skies, seas of waving corn, distant mountains, and gleaming lilies, in a landscape with Lake Gennesaret for its centre, and

to hear with him in the whispering of the reeds the eternal melody of the Sermon on the Mount. (Schweitzer, *Quest of the Historical Jesus*)

Read through Renan's eyes, the Gospels *seem* to offer a historical picture, but it is actually all in the mind of the contemporary reader. Imaginatively Schweitzer can even say that Renan "met" Jesus. For Renan wrote with the gifts and skill of a novelist. Even though he insists "his purpose . . . was purely historical," in his hands the Sermon on the Mount of Matthew's Gospel has the timeless and eternal resonance of poetry. After Renan, why do we need to read the Bible at all, since he provides us with all the poetry we need?

The corrosive effects of nineteenth-century "historical criticism," together with the development of the novel as the major literary genre, brought about the final disintegration of the traditional authority of the biblical canon in modern hermeneutics. From being a branch of theology, hermeneutics had become a scholarly, technical science, and its outcome was either to encapsulate the Bible within the limited, academic world of "biblical criticism," or to consign it finally to the ranks of poetry and world literature, its credentials measured against the (not inconsiderable though hardly sacred) claims of the great fiction of the day. And what of the historical Jesus? Let Schweitzer have the last word on this newly mysterious and elusive figure who simply slips away from the harsh glare of modern hermeneutical inquiry:

We have no terms today which can express what he means for us. He comes to us as one unknown, without a name, as of old, by the lakeside, he came to those men who did not know who he was. He says the same words, "Follow me!" and sets us to those tasks, which he must fulfil in our time. He commands. And to those who hearken to him, whether wise or unwise, he will reveal himself in the peace, the labours, the conflicts and the suffering that they may experience in his fellowship, and as an ineffable mystery they will learn who he is. . . . (Schweitzer, *Quest of the Historical Jesus*)

By a curious paradox, the wheel has come full circle, hermeneutics imposing its circularity again. The losing of the Jesus known through church and theology has taken us back to a primal moment of encounter, two moments of history touching one another, from the disciples of the Gospels to the modern reader. The encounter with Jesus, we would say, has become *existential*— a crucial word in twentieth-century hermeneutics, as we shall see in the next chapter.

4 Wilhelm Dilthey (1833–1911)

A philosopher of history and culture, the German scholar Wilhelm Dilthey cannot be situated easily in any one academic discipline. His vast learning in all branches of the humanities serves to emphasize the *interdisciplinarity* of hermeneutics. The task of interpretation and of understanding it, by the end of the nineteenth century, involved not only theologians but also philosophers, literary critics, sociologists, anthropologists—the list is almost endless.

Dilthey was deeply influenced by the work of Schleiermacher, of whom he wrote a massive *Life*, and "like him, he saw the act of understanding as an attempt to recreate the creative process of the writer or artist" (*Oxford Dictionary of the Christian Church*, 3d ed.). Reading was not merely receptive, but essentially it was as creative as writing itself. Dilthey's basic interest was in exploring *how* we come to know and understand anything, what in philosophy we have called *epistemology*, and this term lies at the very root of his hermeneutics. Beginning his career as a theologian, Dilthey placed hermeneutics within the broad context of the *human sciences*, for which he sought the critical foundations in order to give them credibility alongside the aggressive rise of the *natural sciences* with all their claims for exactitude and precise technical observation. In short, his concern was with *methodology*, or analyzing the means by which we come to understand a text.

Dilthey is most accessible for us in an essay of 1910 entitled "The Development of Hermeneutics," which is reprinted in volume 1 of David Klemm's reader, *Hermeneutical Inquiry* (see

"Recommended Reading" in the Introduction to this book). With him we have a genuinely *universal hermeneutic*, which embraces all of human life and experience. His key category is "life" (*Leben*) or "lived experience" (*Erlebnis*), which he sees as that which is common to all of us, a weaving together of all human activities and experiences. The experience of "humankind" is universal, across all possible cultural and historical barriers. (This is an assumption that is easy to criticize. Do all

> This is an assumption that is easy to criticize. Do all human beings in all times, cultures, and places share a common "lived experience"? What do you think?

human beings in all times, cultures, and places share a common "lived experience"? What do you think?)

For Dilthey, the expressions of our common understanding are in signs, symbols, speech, and writing. The interpreter gains understanding of the writer or text (the "other") by a process of "re-living" (*Nacherleben*) experience on the basis of "empathy" (*Hineinversetzen*). Thus we come to understand, and to understand ourselves, in the *social* activity of reading in interpretive communities, and not through solitary introspection. Learning about our differences from others, we come to learn about ourselves. This requires an act of the *imagination*, a transporting or transposing of oneself into the mind and life of the other. In a statement that anticipates many thinkers in the twentieth century (from Martin Buber's *I and Thou* [1923] to the more recent ethical writings of Immanuel Levinas), Dilthey affirmed that "understanding [*Verstehen*] is a re-discovery of the I and the Thou."

Dilthey is no abstract theoretician. He is concerned with actual experience in what we now would call the social sciences, which he named *Geisteswissenschaften*, which means literally, the science of the mind, or spirit. Like a true hermeneut, he begins with the individual and the particular, but sees this within the whole of culture, emphasizing the "connectedness" of all things.

For Dilthey, to understand a text is, in the first instance, a tracing back to the experience that first brought it into being. To gain understanding is then to move from the particular and to participate in a universal experience and share in broad patterns of intelligibility. With Dilthey, Schleiermacher's pursuit of a universal hermeneutics is expanded into the whole of the human sciences. Dilthey takes us firmly into the twentieth century, which is the subject of our next chapter.

5   Science and Religion

As we have seen in this chapter, science and its claims became crucial for hermeneutics in the nineteenth century. Before we move on, however, we need briefly to qualify what we mean by "science."

The science of the nineteenth century was based on an understanding of the laws of physics usually associated with Isaac Newton (1642–1727), most famous for his "discovery" of the law of gravity. Newtonian physics is based on the principle of cause and effect and on universal, observable laws and principles founded on order and reason. But in the very last year of the nineteenth century, May 18, 1899, to be precise, the scientist Max Planck coined the word "quantum," heralding a new age of physics, which accelerated less than a decade later with Einstein's theory of special relativity.

I am not a scientist, and scientific principles are not directly our concern here, but this *paradigm shift* in scientific thinking, from the *reasoned order* of Newton to the *relativity principle* of Einstein, effected a whole new perspective on the world which would also bring about a profound shift in interpretation theory and hermeneutics. The world, language, and texts were radically destabilized from the notions of order and wholeness, based either on God or on reason, and the new era of relativity takes us into the twentieth century and ultimately into the hermeneutics of *postmodernity* to which our story has been leading for some time. And so we move into chapter 6.

Summary

We might summarize the main points of this chapter as follows:

1. In the nineteenth century, hermeneutics was suspended

between the scientific critical spirit and the residual will to believe.

2. Friedrich Strauss's *Life of Jesus* dissects the Gospel narratives with the tools of modern philosophical investigation and with a pure skepticism.

3. In his quest for the historical Jesus, Renan portrays a Jesus who is a product of the late romantic mind.

4. Wilhelm Dilthey situates hermeneutics within the context of the social sciences. The secularization of hermeneutics is complete.

Activities and Questions

1. Do you think that the radical distinction made by Matthew Arnold between the *literary* (or poetic) and the *scientific* elements in hermeneutics is justified? How would you define these two terms?

2. Compare the hermeneutics of David Friedrich Strauss with those of Thomas Aquinas, and assess, in your own words, the differences between them.

3. Reflect on how far *your* image of the historical Jesus has been formed by the romantic imagination of a writer like Renan and his "followers" in twentieth-century film and literature. (The "Jesus" of Franco Zeffirelli's hugely popular film *Jesus of Nazareth*, for instance, is directly descended from the "pale Galilean" of Renan's *Life of Jesus*.) How, as a reader today, would you set about recovering the "historical Jesus"? Is this even a legitimate quest? What would be your purpose?

4. Wilhelm Dilthey, it has been said, stands between two worlds, the ancient and the modern. Itemize the ways you think that this is true in terms of the hermeneutical task.

5. Do you think that contemporary Christian theology and its hermeneutics have effected the kind of paradigm shifts which have been experienced in science from Newton to Einstein? Is it necessary that they should?

Chapter Six

The Twentieth Century

1 Introduction

With the twentieth century, hermeneutics met the space age and new kinds of fundamentalism beyond the reason of the Enlightenment. It was an age of new mass media, the effect of which on the practice of reading is still hard to assess. It was also a century of unprecedented mass destruction and the fear of nuclear holocaust. Questions were being asked without any means available for providing answers or resolutions. It was an age not of romantic ruins but of jagged, broken fragments and the collapse of dreams, symbolized most poignantly, perhaps, in recent years by the destruction of the twin towers of the World Trade Center in New York—a primitive act effected by the tools of modern science with devastating efficiency.

All this has had its effect on the theory and practice of hermeneutics. Contemplating the work of the German philosopher Martin Heidegger, whom we shall consider briefly later in this chapter, the critic John Caputo now regards hermeneutics as merely an attempt to stick with the original difficulty and confusion of life without seeking resolution or meaning in the chaos. After the massive and systematic scholarly efforts of the nineteenth century, the new hermeneutics is fundamentally unacademic, representing a new approach to the task of understanding, which prefers to let questions hang in the air and resists all easy solutions or answers. The age of reason was over, but this did not mean a return to the former glories of hermeneutics of faith of earlier Christian ages.

2   Karl Barth (1886–1968) and Rudolf Bultmann (1884–1976)

But we must begin the twentieth century with two Protestant theologians who in their different ways are clearly within the traditions that we have been largely following so far—Karl Barth and Rudolf Bultmann. These two near contemporaries dominate German-speaking theology and hermeneutics in the first half of the twentieth century. Karl Barth's work and influence on modern thinking, especially through his massive discussion of Christian doctrine in the *Church Dogmatics*, which he began to publish in 1932 and worked on for most of the rest of his life, is so vast in its extent that we can barely scratch the surface of it here. Born in Basel, Barth spent the years of the First World War as a pastor in Safenwil, Switzerland, having been educated largely in Germany. His reaction to the terrible mass slaughter of the war, and not least the endorsement of the German war effort by his former teachers of theology, led to his first great book, perhaps the most significant for our purposes, his commentary on the Letter to the Romans, the *Römerbrief*. There Barth writes appreciatively but critically of the historical-critical tools of biblical criticism that had been so laboriously developed in the previous century, and finally brushes them aside for a more immediate approach to the Pauline text:

> The Historical-critical Method of Biblical investigation has its rightful place: It is concerned with the preparation of the intelligence—and this can never be superfluous. But, were I driven to choose between it and the venerable doctrine of Inspiration, I should without hesitation adopt the latter, which has a broader, deeper, more important justification. The doctrine of Inspiration is concerned with the labour of apprehending, without which no technical equipment, how-

ever complete, is of any use whatever. (Barth, *Epistle to the Romans*)

It is easy to see here how Barth is a true son of Martin Luther. He sees the Bible as God's freely given revelation, and our part as readers of the Letter to the Romans is to "listen" to the word of God and to respond to it obediently. Barth, like Luther, was above all a preacher. Hermeneutics is central to his theology, because to read the Bible was to open oneself to God's revelation, and this leads to action—the living of the Christian life. In a sense, as we read the word of Scripture, God thereby reads and interprets us and uses us to do his will.

We have seen a certain clear anti-intellectualism in Barth's hermeneutics. Some contemporary scholars, like the English theologian Graham Ward (in his book *Barth, Derrida and the Language of Theology*, 1995) and the American scholar Walter Lowe (in his book *Theology and Difference*, 1993), have seen Karl Barth as anticipating elements of a *postmodern* hermeneutics, and there is some truth in this, as we shall see later on, though his frame of mind is anything but postmodern. For in one way, paradoxically, there simply *is* no hermeneutic in Barth's program, which admits only the "impossible possibility" of faith (reminding us of the man in Mark 9:24 who cried out to Jesus, "I believe; help my unbelief!"). After the elaborate philosophical interpretive programs and scientific definitions of scholars like Schleiermacher and Dilthey, Barth's message is a preacher's cry that radically disturbs all hermeneutics: Listen, against all reason, to the voice of God speaking to us through his Word. He is not all that far from the character in John Steinbeck's novel *East of Eden* (1952) who insists that the Bible is not there to be understood, but to be read and listened to. Too much struggling to understand can actually prevent us from hearing what God is saying to us through its words as a call to action. What Barth is always emphasizing is the chasm that exists between the Word of God and the word of humankind, and thus he restores to the Bible its ancient authority bestriding all concerns of culture, ancient or modern.

And so, as we turn to the New Testament scholar Rudolf Bultmann, it is not very surprising to find that Bultmann seems to doubt if Barth *has* any hermeneutical program at all. If Barth sees our meeting with God as a meeting with the "wholly other," beyond all possible human thought or reason, Bultmann insists on exploring this connecting point between the divine and the human as a meeting of God's self-revelation with our human capacity for understanding.

Thus, in a late essay of 1950 entitled "The Problem of Hermeneutics" (see Klemm, vol. 1), Bultmann situates himself firmly in the intellectual and hermeneutical tradition of Schleiermacher and Dilthey, though with one major difference. Bultmann was deeply influenced also by the German philosopher Martin Heidegger, whose work we will consider briefly in a moment, and by the mode of philosophical thought known as *existentialist*. As a result, his hermeneutics is not so much a program of reconstructing the origins of the text (recall how Schleiermacher requires the reader to "enter into the mind of the author") as it is a delving into the subject matter of the text as it relates to our lives here and now. Bultmann is not really interested in the mind of the apostle Paul! We can put this in another way: for Bultmann the focus of reading is not a reconstructed moment at the very first instant of the text's life (to understand the text is to try and understand what was going on in the mind of Paul or Shakespeare), but rather the present moment of encounter between the text and the reader. The question is, what does the text mean *now* as I read?

There are two important things to be said about this.

1. The process of *demythologizing*. We have already encountered this term in our survey of David Friedrich Strauss (chapter 5). Bultmann does not underestimate the power of myth—indeed, quite the contrary. For him, myths are anything but old legends or mere stories and fables. Myths, rather, are expressions of human "being" in the world. We all live within their terms, and they are changing all the time as culture and society changes. But the ancient mythical world of the New Testament needs to be translated for our time, in a word, demythologized,

so that its nonmythological intention becomes apparent for *us*, "existentially." Bultmann might say that most of us no longer live, for example, in a world in which illness is perceived as demon possession. In order to understand what is actually being said in the healing miracles of the Gospels, therefore, we need to translate them into terms that are more culturally accessible to us. This is not at all, it should be stressed, to dismiss the importance of what is being said about Jesus in these narratives. It is a process not actually that different from that of Strauss in *Das Leben Jesu*.

2. Through his focus on the subject matter of the text, Bultmann is concerned to unveil what it says to us regarding the manner of our self-understanding. Hermeneutics, in other words, is about discovering who we are and how we understand ourselves—in short, about exploring the meaning of human existence.

It has sometimes been said that Bultmann is ultimately not all that interested in the biblical text, but only in what it says. His approach is the precise opposite of Barth in this respect. Barth keeps our attention on the text in front of us. Bultmann moves through the text to the subject matter that lies, in a sense, behind it.

Learning from Heidegger, Bultmann defines two modes of human existence, the authentic and the inauthentic. Authentically we *gain* ourselves within our understanding of "being" (*Dasein*). This is a German term from Heidegger, which we will look at in a moment. Inauthentically, we *lose* ourselves. What has all this got to do with reading the Bible? Bultmann would direct us back immediately to Mark 8:35–36:

> For those who want to save their life will lose it, and those who lose their life for my sake, and for the sake of the gospel, will save it. For what will it profit them to gain the whole world and forfeit their life?

This is a perfect statement of authentic existence, translated (or demythologized) by Bultmann into the existential philosophy of Martin Heidegger.

3   Martin Heidegger (1889–1976)

Heidegger is one of the most difficult, controversial, and important thinkers of the twentieth century, but a survey of hermeneutics cannot avoid an acknowledgment of his central place in hermeneutical theory and understanding. With him we move on, now, from the world of theologians and biblical critics like Barth and Bultmann into the wider world of philosophical and literary reflection. Heidegger is *difficult*, because his German language is highly idiosyncratic, an instrument used to delve *behind* thinking and concepts of thought into their very origins. He tends to avoid the technical language of philosophy, but uses words in an idiosyncratic way that makes translation extremely difficult. Heidegger is *controversial* because he was, as rector of Freiburg University, a member of the Nazi party, and the debate about this has continued to rage through the years. The point is, how seriously can we take the thought of a man who is ethically so problematic? Yet he is *important*, because no thinker in the West in the twentieth century can finally avoid the implications of what he said and wrote. We have noted how important he was for Rudolf Bultmann. Here I will confine myself to two further points—but don't imagine for one moment that this sums up "Heidegger." That would require at least another book, and Heidegger's philosophy lies far beyond our present scope!

1. So far we have been assuming that the fundamental question in hermeneutics is something like "How do we come to understand texts?" Largely speaking, the varieties of hermeneutics we looked at have all tried to offer some kind of answer to this question. Heidegger goes back one step farther to the question of "being" itself. The crucial word in his early masterwork *Being and Time* (1927) is the German *Dasein*, usually left untranslated because it is, essentially, untranslatable. *Dasein* refers not to my being or any specific "being." *Dasein* is simply "being there" in the universe. It is, indeed, a word on the very edge of linguistic possibility itself. This is Heidegger's intention, since his concern is with "the

ontological foundation of modern hermeneutical theory" (Klemm), that is, its very origins. And so he goes behind the question, to "being" itself. With Heidegger, hermeneutics moves far beyond the business of textual interpretation. It returns in a curious way (another hermeneutic circle?), via philosophy and, by implication, to the most profound questions of theology—hermeneutics and theology are met again. Heidegger, however, would never have described himself as a theologian. As a good hermeneut he was more interested in breaking down the limitations of disciplines, beyond theology or philosophy. Behind him lies another thinker, Edmund Husserl, who sought to free philosophical thinking from all systems and speculations in a return to "things in themselves." The shift is in a sense away from *epistemology* (a term we have encountered frequently since our look at Kant) and toward *ontology*.

2. In his later writings Heidegger adopts a poetic, even mystical, tone. More than in texts he is profoundly interested in *language* itself, so that one commentator, Joseph Kockelmans, has rather cryptically commented that "[l]anguage is no longer just a tool, but it itself speaks" (Kockelmans, *On the Truth of Being*). Heidegger almost seems to suggest that language has a divine rather than a human origin, but he is not here speaking of Scripture. Rather, language expresses "being" itself, far beyond the limits of human intentions, so that hermeneutics or "interpretation is the meditative, even poetic, process of listening and giving voice to the linguistic (and hence finite) appearance of being" (Klemm, *Hermeneutical Inquiry*, vol. 1).

Heidegger is, curiously, at once both very difficult and very simple to understand. With him we find ourselves on the very edge of language and thought—hence his rather mystical tone. He transforms the nature of philosophical inquiry in the twentieth century, but then moves beyond philosophy to an interplay with text (he was a great reader of poetry, especially the German romantic poet Friedrich Hölderlin) and language that remains rooted in history and yet allows "conversations" with matters of infinite concern, with Being itself.

4   Hans-Georg Gadamer (1900–2002)

In a world that is perpetually being threatened with disintegration and fragmentation, one of the obsessions of the modern mind since romanticism has been with wholeness and the recovery of a vision of life that embraces all things, rather as Christianity had done in the Christendom of the Middle Ages. In a way, Heidegger's whole life was devoted to exploring the coherence of "Being" and the connectedness of all things. With Hans-Georg Gadamer we have a hermeneut par excellence, whose long working life (he was still lecturing at one hundred years old!) was devoted to emphasizing the universality of hermeneutics, a theme we have been pursuing since we looked at Schleiermacher's work.

In 1966, Gadamer wrote an essay entitled "The Universality of the Hermeneutical Problem" (reprinted in Klemm, vol. 1), but his chief claim to fame rests on his massive book *Wahrheit und Methode* (*Truth and Method*), published in 1960 and deeply influenced by Heidegger. An essentially conservative thinker, Gadamer offers us here perhaps the most systematic survey of hermeneutics in the twentieth century, its title indicating his dialogue between the claims of "truth" on the one hand and the processes of "method" on the other—a return to what should by now be to you a familiar pattern in hermeneutical thinking as it exists between an absolute demand (whether of God or *Dasein*) and the relentless, systematic application of methods and processes. In short, Gadamer returns us to the question of the hermeneutics of faith and the hermeneutics of suspicion, and he suggests that, ultimately, in our reading we have to decide between one and the other. Indeed, it has often been remarked that his book ought more properly to have been entitled "*Truth 'or' Method*." For him, the final word is always with "truth."

Like Dilthey before him, Gadamer cannot be contained within any one academic discipline. His hermeneutics voyage across the seas of philosophy, theology, classics, literary criticism, and even legal theory. A student of Heidegger (who supervised his *Habilitationschrift* on the philosophy of Plato), and influenced also by Bultmann, Gadamer exhibits many of the traits of his teacher. Above all, his suspicion is primarily of the modern age itself, with its division of learning and understanding into separate and often discrete categories or disciplines (we sometimes say, "I am a theologian, not a philosopher," or, "I am a literary critic, not a New Testament critic," for example), at the danger of losing our sense of the whole of life. Gadamer tries to see things from all perspectives. It is a classic hermeneutic move, another "circle," to remind us to see the particular from the perspective of the whole, and to articulate the whole by the careful examination of particulars.

The mythologies of specific disciplines, and we should include biblical criticism among them, become distorted and myopic in their relation to the world unless they are seen within wider, more universal claims. Thus, the true hermeneut is faced with the impossible task of mastering all "disciplines" (and not all of us are blessed with Gadamer's extraordinary, and intellectually productive, longevity!). Yet at the same time Gadamer is no pedant making impossible demands on his students. Early on in *Truth and Method* he introduces the concept of "play" as central to the experience of truth. His discussion is rather complex, but it may be boiled down to three points that can quite easily be understood. (Think of any game you might be involved in, either as a child or as a member of a college team.)

1. The purpose of play is fulfilled only when the player "loses" himself or herself utterly in the game. The game has to become a "world."
2. To be effective, play has to be taken absolutely seriously. We all know what it is like to play a game, whether of football or cards, in which another player does not "play seriously." It takes all the real fun out of it!
3. When we are playing a game properly, and are wholly absorbed in it, it may become a "sphere of disclosure" in

which we realize and learn something new, or see it in a new way. That is why games are so important—and they work only when we play by the rules.

These three points maybe transferred quite easily to the experience of reading a book. When we are reading "seriously" we "lose ourselves" in the book, we take its world absolutely seriously (even though we "know" it is fictitious), and serious disclosures do often take place. This might be true of a novel, or it might be true of the Gospels, which one eminent New Testament scholar has recently described as "true fiction" (Douglas A. Templeton, *The New Testament as True Fiction*, 1999). If one needed further assurance of the seriousness of the business we are engaged in as "play," we might also recall Hamlet's strategy to "catch the conscience" of Claudius by means of a play within the play—"The Mousetrap."

Finally, Gadamer warns us, when reading hermeneuts like Schleiermacher or Dilthey, of the danger of assuming that we read back "historically" in texts like the Bible from a position of objectivity. That is, we tend to assume that our position is a stable and clear one, and that any instability lies either in the text or in the processes of understanding. But Gadamer reminds us that we ourselves live and read from within the flux of history, and our vantage point of today is no more absolute or objective in its assumptions than any other. We are, in a way, no better (or worse) than earlier readers, and like them we have our strengths and weaknesses, our strong points and our naïvetés. Gadamer, then, is highly suspicious of any claim to know the mind of the author better than the author does himself or herself. What a presumption! Rather, any act of historical understanding is itself historical, and all our interpretations are themselves part of the stream of history itself. We can have no privileged perspectives.

5 Paul Ricoeur (1913–)

The prodigious output of the French philosopher and critic Paul Ricoeur remains still unfinished, as he continues to write and publish. If Gadamer and Ricoeur are anything to go by, hermeneutics are very good for health and a productive long life! Ricoeur, whose academic career has been split between France and the U.S.A., has described himself as "a philosopher who identifies himself with the so-called hermeneutic school of thought" (LaCocque and Ricoeur, *Thinking Biblically*). Self-consciously working in the great tradition of nineteenth-century hermeneutics, Ricoeur, like Gadamer, is a scholar who ranges across many intellectual disciplines in his hermeneutical inquiries.

In an early book entitled *The Symbolism of Evil* (1960), Ricoeur establishes that evil is not directly accessible, but is perceived only in its expressions and their effects. In other words the very notion of "evil" itself requires a process of interpretation, a hermeneutics, for us to identify it. Yet, if Ricoeur is a hermeneut through and through, and interpretation is a universal necessity in the absence of "direct access" to, say, the absolute fact of evil, there is another side to him, which is summed up in a famous sentence that appears toward the end of *The Symbolism of Evil*: "Beyond the desert of criticism we wish to be called again."

Yet the desert of intellectual travail must be journeyed through and crossed if we are to hear the voice calling us back: again suspicion and faith. Throughout his work Ricoeur respects both the philosophical text, in all its rigor, and the poetic text, with its melody and intuition. They stand apart, and only in their differences do they speak to one another. Having crossed the desert, with the hard labor that that requires, we may expect to enter into what Ricoeur names as a "second naïveté"—a simplicity of understanding born of wisdom and hard work.

Many of Ricoeur's books deal directly with the business of biblical interpretation, addressing directly such fundamental issues as revelation, authority, and the nature of the "sacred text." For example, he distinguishes between the Qur'an as the sacred text for Muslims, and the Bible, wherein "it is not the text that is sacred but the one about which is spoken" (*Figuring the Sacred*). Then, after his initial investment in the sacred subject matter of the biblical text, Ricoeur is free to apply rigorous procedures of interpretation in the reading of it. In a sense, he is like the hermeneuts of old, who began their reading of the Bible with prayer and devotion. He is careful to see its language not as *literal* (which reduces to a single meaning in the manner of science), but rather as *figurative* (which recognizes many voices and levels of meaning working together to create new meanings and insights).

Ricoeur, we see, in a sense stretches back beyond the Reformation, to earlier modes of Christian hermeneutics characteristic of Augustine, the church fathers, and the medieval theologians, who saw may levels of meaning in the biblical texts all working together.

If Heidegger and Gadamer seem to take hermeneutics away from what had always been its primary concern, the interpretation of texts, to questions of philosophy, language, and ontology, Ricoeur returns us directly to the primary issues of textual interpretation. Furthermore, his is at heart a traditional hermeneutics of faith, yet one that is also situated in the Enlightenment and post-Enlightenment story that we have been following. This balance is most delicately expressed in one of Ricoeur's more difficult but crucially important philosophical texts, *Soi même comme un autre* (*Oneself as Another*) (1992). The passage requires, and repays, careful reading, so take some time to absorb it:

> The ten studies that make up this work assume the bracketing, conscious and resolute, of the convictions that bind me to biblical faith. I do not claim that at the deep level of motivations these convictions remain without any effect on the interest that I take in this or that problem, even in the overall problematic of the self. [This is the subject of *Oneself as Another*.] But I think that I have presented to my readers arguments alone, which do not assume any commitment from the reader to reject, accept, or suspend anything with regard to biblical faith. It will be observed that this asceticism of the argument, which marks, I believe, all my philosophical work, leads to a type of philosophy from which the actual mention of God is absent and in which the question of God, as a philosophical question, itself remains in a suspicion that could be called agnostic. (Ricoeur, *Oneself as Another*)

This is a delicate and nuanced summation of the task of the contemporary Christian hermeneut. Ricoeur admits his "biblical faith" and the rooted convictions that lie at its heart. At the same time, "textual interpretation" demands a rigorous discipline, which involves, as far as possible, the suspension of the prejudices and preconceptions inherent in any uncritical "faith." *Oneself as Another*, as a rigorous investigation into philosophical questions, must "bracket out" the requirements of his convictions about the Bible and indeed his discussion of God, while at the same time these convictions actually lie at the secret heart of his whole endeavor. (Indeed, Ricoeur's argument is rather similar to that of Coleridge in his *Confessions of an Inquiring Spirit*, and it may be helpful to go back again and remind ourselves of that work, which we discussed in chapter 4, before going any farther.)

> Indeed, Ricoeur's argument is rather similar to that of Coleridge in his *Confessions of an Inquiring Spirit*, and it may be helpful to go back again and remind ourselves of that work, which we discussed in chapter 4, before going any farther.

Hermeneutics does not preach; nor do Ricoeur's texts. The reader must be free to make a judgment one way or another. The "asceticism" of his argument lies precisely in *not* allowing religious beliefs to skew the text of the reading. But the unspoken implication of the final sentence must be that God, or indeed the Bible, is never very far away in Ricoeur's work, and proper hermeneutical inquiry will lead us back to the unspoken word that lies at its heart.

6 Toward the Postmodern: Jacques Derrida (1930–)

What follows will be little more than a note or an addendum to this chapter, as it looks forward to the discussion of contemporary hermeneutics in the next chapter. However, the contemporary interpreter needs at least some sense of what the term "postmodern" implies (I will not say "means") and how it affects, or possibly even invalidates, the project of hermeneutics as we have followed it up to the still-ongoing work of Paul Ricoeur. At the same time, the term "postmodern" is itself now becoming rather outdated since its heyday in the 1970s and 1980s, and the fear and disapproval that its youthful proponents then instilled in more conservative critics has been replaced by an almost staid seniority that is rather unwilling to admit that it is no longer young, and hermeneutics, as always, has begun to move on in different directions.

Though employed in various, often rather vague, ways and in many fields (it was first used as a term in architecture), the word "postmodern" is basically employed to describe the cultural emergence, or perhaps decline, from the "modern" age of Enlightenment and post-Enlightenment thought. Like hermeneutics itself, it is entirely interdisciplinary, being used in rather different ways in architecture, music, literature, and even theology. It acknowledges the breakdown of *essentialist categories*—that is, that we can ever reach or speak of the essence of anything, whether that is God or merely language itself. Nothing can be spoken of in itself. Postmodernity is characterized by notions of *relativity* and a suspicion of paradox. Jacques Derrida, the French thinker who more than anyone else seems to epitomize the term (it can hardly be described as a movement), delights in coining words that are not real dictionary words but rather exist *between* words, *deconstructing* what we assume to be the structures of language and reference. The best-known example of this is his "word" *différance*, which is not a word you will find in any French dictionary. It is a word suspended between two actual words, to "differ" and to "defer." All meaning is in difference; all meaning is deferred.

A hugely important figure in the gallery of postmodernism is the rather enigmatic Swiss linguist Ferdinand de Saussure (1857–1913). A brief look at his work is important for our work in hermeneutics, as he is perhaps the single most important modern figure in the field of understanding the nature of language and how we use it.

In a course of lectures delivered in 1911, which he himself never published, Saussure revolutionized how we understand the workings of language, and therefore, by extension, how we understand texts. The story has been told often, and I do not intend to repeat it at length here. (You might follow it up in Jonathan Culler's excellent brief study simply entitled *Saussure*, 1976.) At its heart is the understanding of language simply as a play of differences. The word "dog" is understood as referring to my furry little friend with four legs only because it is *not* a "cat." (Remember that in post-modernity there are no essences, and that includes language.) Words do not actually refer to anything except by mutual agreement and because they are different from other words. There is no intrinsic link between the letters and sound "dog" and Rover over there in the garden, and you could just as well say *"chien"* (if you were French), or whatever you say if you are Chinese or Hungarian. In the end, as long as we understand each other any word will do.

> Remember that in postmodernity there are no essences, and that includes language.

I have labored this point a bit because it is important to appreciate how Saussure's rather academic researches in linguistics feed into the traumatic events of so-called *deconstruction*, that is, the critical overturning of all the structures and hierarchies on which we have built beliefs and belief systems in culture. The Frankfurt philosopher Jürgen Habermas has expressed it in this way; read the following passage carefully:

> The rebellious labour of deconstruction aims indeed at dismantling smuggled-in basic conceptual hierarchies, at overthrowing foundational relationships and conceptual relations of domination, such as those between speech and writing, the intelligible and the sensible, nature and culture, inner and outer, mind and matter, male and female. Logic and rhetoric constitute one of these conceptual pairs. Derrida is particularly interested in standing the primacy of logic over rhetoric, canonized since Aristotle, on its head. (Habermas, *The Philosophical Discourse of Modernity*)

Postmodernism, it seems, is the final abandonment of logic and reason and their long reign in the ordered world of hermeneutics. Like Gadamer, Derrida refers to the concept of play, but it is far from the sedate, well-ruled game of Gadamer. Derrida's post-modern play is full of *jouissance*, tricks and blind alleys. Two things need to be borne in mind at this point.

1. If Derrida is more concerned with rhetoric than the demands of logic (and reason), we need to remind ourselves that Plato, for one, deeply distrusted rhetoric and explains why at some length in his dialogue called the *Phaedrus*. For the rhetorician is not ultimately concerned with the truth of anything, but only with persuading you that something is true. Rhetoric is the art of persuasion. If I can persuade you to believe that the moon is made of cheese, then I am a successful rhetorician, and the actual constitution of the moon is irrelevant! Think for a moment what the prioritizing of rhetoric means for the status of texts and their truth claims. In short, are we just being conned by texts all the time?

2. Deconstruction is not something that you consciously *do*. People sometimes talk about a deconstructive reading of a text (say a Gospel) as an alternative to a historical reading, or a formalist reading. But Derrida's point is that texts themselves are inherently deconstructive of the very meanings that they might seem to promote and embody. Words and texts will play with any meanings that you might seek to impose on them. Deconstruction is the ultimate acknowledgment of the age-old adage that we encountered in chapter 1 in our discussion of Humpty Dumpty. We never quite say what we mean and we never quite mean what we say.

For some people all this means a wonderful new freedom. Powerful texts like the Bible have a history of readings that may be marvelous for some folk, but for others they may have meant repression and subordination. Feminist hermeneutics, for example, flourished in its release from the patriarchal structures—men dominating women—inherent in biblical culture and the long history of male-dominated biblical interpretation. If you think about it, there has not been *one* woman hermeneut mentioned in this book until now. Well, don't blame me personally. It has not been for the want of looking! There just aren't any, or at least any who have been allowed to be heard through publication or public position, until the postmodern and deconstructive turn began to allow them to speak. The result has been such works as the Dutch critic Mieke Bal's searing rereadings of the book of Judges, which *deconstruct* their narratives of patriarchal male power through a *countercoherence* perceived in hitherto neglected female voices in the text.

But for others, postmodernism means just chaos, values lost in a sea of relativities (what would Einstein have thought?), readings in which anything goes, and, above all, confirmation of what the German thinker Friedrich Nietzsche proclaimed in the nineteenth century as the "death of God" (*The Gay Science*, 1882). If all readings are relative, how are we to prefer one above another, and who now arbitrates between what is right and what is wrong, between good and bad? In a famous essay entitled "Is There a Text in This Class?" (1980) the American critic Stanley Fish addressed the question as to whether in the postmodern sea of indeterminacy we could even speak of actual texts at all anymore, as they were drowned in the endless babble of claims and counterclaims. The question, Fish recounts, was asked by a student of literature, who went on, "I mean, in this class do we believe in poems and things, or is it just us?" His reply was that there certainly are texts, but they exist within interpretive communities, and their "meanings" emerge only within situations and are never absolute. Fish's argument for textual indeterminacy (or we might call it interpretive or hermeneutical freedom)—which is not at all the same as unintelligibility—is made in opposition to the position of a more conservative American hermeneut, E. D. Hirsch Jr., who defines a text in his book *Validity in Interpretation* (1967) as "an entity which always remains the same from one moment to the next." (The irony is, of course, that Fish's essay has remained pretty stable and authoritative in the classrooms of literature departments for over twenty years!)

But Nietzsche was, after all, quite mad, at least at the end of his life. Does this mean, then, that now we are *all* mad, or at least drowning in the bottomless seas of postmodernism? How can we trust anything anymore—least of all that ancient text of power, the Bible? Derrida puts the matter before us rather ponderously in his early work *Of Grammatology* (1967; transl. into English, 1976):

> Language itself is menaced in its very life, helpless, adrift in the threat of limitlessness brought back to its own finitude at the very moment when its limits seem to disappear, when it ceases to be self-assured, contained, and *guaranteed* by the infinite signified which seemed to exceed it. (Derrida, *Of Grammatology*)

For "infinite signified" we might here read "God." In the hermeneutics of postmodernity there is no god to guarantee meaning (or at least no god as understood by the term *theism*), and there is no reason either. There are no essences and nothing essential. There is nothing but instability and play, a playtime without responsibility. There is, it seems, no point of reference *outside* the text by which to interpret it. There is, perhaps, nothing outside the text *at all*. The text is, at best, self-authenticating. Or perhaps language is *menaced in its very life* and seems doomed to implode into meaninglessness.

Postmodernism, it is sometimes said, aspires in an almost mystical way toward a state of pure consciousness, free from physical, linguistic constraints. But we need to be very careful to distinguish a proper or genuine mysticism from the terrifying condition that we seem to welcome on all sides and that we might call the realm of *cyberspace*. For in the cyberspace of "information technology," a kingdom that is rapidly threatening to overwhelm the world of texts and books, we do not have to be responsible for our bodies, or even for who we are. There is no limit, no fixed identity (as long as you know your password), no god, and the cowboys run riot. No one rules in a game without rules.

But . . . but, even in the world of postmodernity, texts themselves have "bodies" and forms, which make their demands on us. Christianity, which has been our primary concern in this book, is an *incarnational* religion—a body lies at its very heart. And we ourselves do have bodies, and mutual responsibilities thereby. In the next chapter, then, we will return to the body of the text and the claims it makes on us and we on it.

If postmodernism poses the question to the interpreter of how to legitimate one text in preference to another, then, equally, it poses the problem, how to remain a responsible reader.

Summary

We might summarize the main points of this chapter as follows:

1. Karl Barth cuts through hermeneutical problems with his "dialectical theology" and restores authority to the biblical text.
2. Rudolf Bultmann joins his hermeneutics with an existentialist philosophy, which underlies his program of demythologizing.
3. Martin Heidegger addresses the question of *Dasein*, "being there," and digs under the hermeneutical questions to the roots beneath, thereby reintroducing theology, as it were, by the back door.
4. The universality of hermeneutics is affirmed by Gadamer in this book *Truth and Method*.
5. Paul Ricoeur's contemporary hermeneutics return us to some of the basic issues in Christian interpretation of the Bible with which we began.
6. Postmodernity—the end or a new beginning?

Activities and Questions

1. Who is more relevant for us today, Barth or Bultmann?
2. In what sense do you think that Martin Heidegger was moving *back* to an earlier form of hermeneutics that celebrated the Bible as the immediate word of God? In what sense was he radically new?
3. Compare the hermeneutics of Gadamer regarding the reader and history with those of Eichhorn and Semler (chapter 4). Do you think that we now have special privileges as readers

over the more "primitive" peoples of the earlier culture of the eighteenth century? If so, what are they? (The point is, do hermeneutics *develop*, or do they merely *change*?)

4. Do you see "postmodernism," as we have briefly looked at it in this chapter, as an end or as a new beginning for hermeneutics? How might a "postmodern reader" approach the Bible? (You might find *The Postmodern Bible Reader*, edited by David Jobling, Tina Pippin, and Ronald Schliefer, a very useful guide as you think about this question.)

5. In what ways do you think that computers, the Internet, and information technology are affecting the hermeneutical questions we have been wrestling with in this book? What are the *positive* and the *negative* aspects of this question? You might also consider how our *writing* as well as our *reading* habits have been affected by these technological developments.

Chapter Seven

Varieties of Postmodern Hermeneutics

This final chapter will address a number of hermeneutical issues that face us today. As was suggested in the last chapter, the time has probably now come to recognize that postmodernity itself has already become something of a historical term, and although its long shadow will be with us for some time to come, hermeneutics has already moved on in its restless search. We have seen how at the beginning of the twentieth century Karl Barth could seem to be anticipating certain characteristics of the postmodern, and in some respects this is the case, for both Barth and the postmodern constitute radical turns from the whole Enlightenment movement and a disregard for the elaborate structures and claims of historical criticism. On the other hand, nothing could be farther than Barth from the relativities of postmodern hermeneutics, and their similarities rest in their responding to the social and cultural upheavals of a century that was unprecedented in mechanized violence and bloodshed. As always, hermeneutics is sensitive to all forms of change and technological developments.

This book has been very focused on the interpretation of the Bible, although it has not attempted to offer a history of biblical hermeneutics as such. That can be found elsewhere, in the work of scholars like Robert Grant or Robert Morgan. (Their books are mentioned in the list of Recommended Reading on pp. 4–6). Nor has it offered a history of the development of literary criticism and theory, especially as this became more self-conscious in the second half of the twentieth century. Both of these fields, however, have been ever present in our discussions. The Bible has been largely at the center of our attention because it has been by far the single most important text around which the issues of hermeneutics have revolved. Whether this will always be so is impossible to predict, and you will have noticed that the Bible was less in evidence in the previous chapter, which dealt with the twentieth century.

But the primary themes of this book have been the nature of text and textuality, and the nature of reading as a process. This investigation has been necessarily interdisciplinary, and has plunged from time to time into fairly demanding philosophical arguments, as well as theology, linguistics, poetics, and so on. Above all, I hope that it has become clear that for anyone who sets out to study the Christian tradition (although it is equally true of the Jewish and Islamic traditions, in different ways) we cannot imagine that hermeneutics is an optional extra. The business of "interpretation" lies at its very heart.

In this chapter we shall address a number of themes and issues that are especially pressing for hermeneutics at the present time. They do not pretend to be comprehensive, and within time some will need to be deleted and others added. Such is the restless nature of the hermeneutical enterprise.

1   The Bible as Literature/the Bible in Literature

The poet T. S. Eliot in his 1935 essay "Religion and Literature" stated that he did not believe that you could read the Bible purely as literature. It is a sacred text. Eliot makes his point very carefully:

> The Bible has had a *literary* influence upon English Literature *not* because it has been considered as literature, but because it has been considered as the report of the word of God. And the fact that men of letters [sic] now discuss it as

"literature" probably indicates the end of the its "literary" influence. (Eliot, *Selected Essays*)

It is nevertheless the case that there is wonderful literature in the Bible, in both prose and verse. At the same time, the Bible has permeated Western literature like no other text, so that even today it is, arguably, one of the most powerful *cultural*, if not religious, texts in our society. (Only think how Hollywood blockbuster films like *Terminator II* or *Unforgiven* are soaked in biblical images and even biblical language.)

The relationship between the Bible and the rest of literature remains a close, if often uncomfortable, one. Of course the Bible is literature, and yet at the same time, as we have seen, it is set apart in the Western tradition from all other literature, for better or for worse, and how we read it remains a problem. During thirty years of postmodern "theory," it has been notable ho of the leading postmodern thinkers—Derrida is the most o example—are returning to ancient hermeneutical ways in demonstrably rabbinic readings of texts, which seem to suggest a close connection between postmodern and ancient, often Jewish, hermeneutics of the kind that we briefly reviewed in chapter 2. But this only seems to serve to indicate that more or less all our insights into the process of reading arise, in some sense, from our encounters with the biblical texts of the Judaeo-Christian tradition.

And what now of the status of the Bible, and of its authority in an age when the power and authority of the churches and religious institutions seems to be perpetually declining? Was Coleridge right, that there are texts that somehow, mysteriously "find me at greater depths of my being"? Does this effect have to be something to do with theology or religion? It is certainly the case that the influence of the Bible on modern literature is as powerful as ever. For example, some of the greatest of twentieth-century novels, from the writings of Thomas Mann to D. H. Lawrence and John Steinbeck, have drawn directly from the great narratives in the book of Genesis, and it may well be that reading these works of literature is now the best way of recovering a living Bible. In other words, we may now have moved beyond the great age of philosophical hermeneutics and historical criticism (from which we can still learn a great deal, as we have seen), and, after post-modernism, we may now need to have the courage to return to the great stories via contemporary poets and writers of fiction.

Here is an example of what I mean. John Steinbeck's great novel *East of Eden* (1952) is an allegory that retells some of the stories of the early chapters of Genesis in the context of settlers in California in the late nineteenth and early twentieth centuries. Allegory has always been present in both Jewish and Christian reading of Scripture, and Steinbeck continues the midrashic tradition in his novel. Entering into the self-consuming world of his book is to reengage with the story of the fall and the ancient rivalries between the brothers Cain and Abel, and Jacob and Esau. Via the powerful drama of Steinbeck's narrative we may be led back to a recovery of the primal authority of the narratives of Genesis, schooled in a way of reading a fictional narrative that is every bit as valid in its understanding of the nature of the biblical text as the hermeneutics that require a more historical and overtly theological approach.

I would go so far as to say that *East of Eden* ought to be compulsory reading in the curriculum of every seminary and college class that studies the Old Testament.

2 Liberation and Responsibility

In the last chapter we looked briefly at an example of feminist hermeneutics in the work of Mieke Bal. There are also other forms of "liberation" hermeneutics linked to varieties of oppression—race, the poor, children, religious minorities, and so on. Indeed, we might refer back to Martin Luther in this regard, when he speaks of Holy Scripture as the best of books "abounding in comfort under all afflictions and trials." But at the same time, what has often been brought to our attention when such oppressed groups read a powerful text like the Bible is that it can work just as easily for ill as for good. It can be an instrument of oppression as well as an instrument of liberation. This is true of other texts as well; *The Communist Manifesto*, by Marx and Engels, would be an example.

The point is made clearly in Margaret Atwood's 1985 novel *The Handmaid's Tale*, which presents us with a nightmare society of the future based on biblical themes from Genesis (or is it a kind of parable of the present?), in which women of childbearing age are kept as "handmaids" by powerful men in an attempt to provide them with children in a world threatened with sterility. The handmaids are allowed no access to dangerous reading matter (to read, after all, is to empower and encourage us to think for ourselves), and, above all, to the Bible, which is described as "an incendiary device." For who knows what they would make of it if they got their hands on it? The women's only access to Scripture is through readings from it by their male Commander. Atwood's point is that this is exactly how most women through the ages have been given the Bible, under the control of a firm patriarchal direction that never allows them to check its interpretive voice against their own reading of the text. In one passage the women are read to during their mealtime from the Beatitudes of Matthew 5. The opening sentence is significant: "For lunch it was the Beatitudes." They are "fed" the text by the reader on the record.

> Blessed be this, blessed be that. They played it from a disc, the voice was a man's. *Blessed be the poor in spirit, for theirs is the kingdom of heaven. Blessed are the merciful. Blessed are the meek. Blessed are the silent.* I knew they made that up, I knew it was wrong, and they left things out too, but there was no way of checking. (Margaret Atwood, *The Handmaid's Tale*)

We can see what a revolution it was when Luther gave each of his students a printed, standard Bible and told each of them to read it, verify, and check for themselves. Texts are dangerous (and especially this text), and to read is to be empowered, and therefore to become responsible.

What can hermeneutics, as we have been studying it, contribute to the *ethical* dilemmas posed when texts of power become texts of terror? Can we stand neutral, as merely "academic" interpreters? Is hermeneutics necessarily a political activity? We need to be aware that such a pernicious political program as apartheid in South Africa had its beginnings in a particular biblical hermeneutics that saw all things created as distinct under God, their differences to be clearly acknowledged. This includes the color of our skin. Politics inevitably imposed a hierarchy on this—male above female, white above black, and so on. It is why also the voices of poets and writers continue to be so important in all "liberation" movements of the poor and oppressed. To be able to read is to begin to think and therefore to speak—and therefore *how* we read and relate to texts is crucial for our very human nature and its freedom.

3   Politics and Postcolonialism

The theme of political interpretation is continued with the growing literature and criticism from "postcolonial" voices in countries across the world emerging into independence after the collapse of the European empires of the nineteenth and twentieth centuries. Awareness of texts and the spread of education have placed hermeneutics at the center of dynamic explorations of the condition of peoples whose ancient cultures were traumatized by the imposition of European languages, culture, and literatures on them, and above all by the coming of the Bible in the hands of missionaries and administrators who saw it as the Word of God bringing the light of the text to the "heathen in their blindness."

Novels such as Ngũgĩ wa Thiong'o's *Devil on the Cross* (1982), written behind the bars of a Kenyan political prison where the author was being held without trial, searingly overturn traditional Western assumptions about the biblical narratives from cultures where they have often (though not always) been the accompaniment of cultural and social oppression. In his parable of the experience of a young African girl, Ngũgĩ uses biblical narratives to expose the evils of capitalism and colonial oppression, which often work against traditional readings and associations in a society that has not been immersed for two thousand years in the Christian hermeneutical patterns that we have been studying. The novel opens with a searing apocalyptic image that serves to remind us that the powerful imagery of the book of Revelation can take on a whole new life when severed from the ancient Christian associations within which it was originally written. Revelation, after all, was itself, among other things, a grand political vision related to the Roman Empire. What does it mean for us to transfer this energy to the more recent British Empire (or perhaps the economic empire of the United States of America in even more recent history)?

Critical books such as R. S. Sugirtharajah's recent *Postcolonial Criticism and Biblical Interpretation* (2002) have begun to explore biblical hermeneutics in the light of such postcolonial voices and literature. In his Introduction, Sugirtharajah recounts the story of how British colonial expansion was justified in its day in the light of the text from Genesis 28:14: "You shall spread abroad to the west and to the east and to the north and to the south." In other words, the injunction given to Jacob by the Lord after his dream of the ladder is simply transferred to the British acquisition of lands in India, Africa, and elsewhere, with all the economic wealth that this implied, with the further assumption that "all the families of the earth shall be blessed in you and in your offspring"(Gen. 28:14). For the British conquerors the biblical text seemed to give unexceptionable approval to their action.

We might also recall that apartheid in South Africa arose, to some extent at least, from biblical criticism and interpretation. In the postcolonial era of the present day it is easy to see how a very different hermeneutic pertains, and how not only is the Bible to be read in a different way in the light of political and social experience, but the power of the new reader must be turned against old prejudices that were once regarded as unquestioned truths.

4   From Intertextuality to Film, Art, and the Body

We have seen how, from the earliest days of the Christian Bible, its status as a "sacred text" has set it apart from all other literature. At some times a hermeneut like Martin Luther would simply exclude all other reading for the Christian, while at others a universal hermeneutic would place it in the context of all world literature, though even there it might hold a unique place described by the translators of the King James Bible of 1611 as "a tree, or rather a whole paradise of trees of life, which bring forth fruit every month, and the fruit thereof is for meat, and the leaves for medicine." What is quite clear, however, is that texts do not live in isolation from one another and that to read one text is a kind of gateway into all other texts that have gone before and that will come after it. In whatever sense we may regard it as the original word of God, as literature the Bible did not spring up out of nothing, but from other more ancient texts, many of them now lost and forgotten. Within its pages are countless conversations between books so that, as we saw in chapter 2, much of the New Testament is a kind of commentary on parts of the earlier Hebrew Bible, and this process has continued throughout the history of literature. In A. S. Byatt's novel *Babel Tower*, one of the characters, Frederica, who is a teacher of literature, writes:

> The narrative of the Novel, in its high days, was built on, out of, and in opposition to the narrative of the one Book, the source of all Books, the Bible. Both [E. M.] Forster and [D. H.] Lawrence use for the joining of lovers the old Biblical symbol of God's covenant between Heaven and Earth, the rainbow, even though Forster's rainbow is also a simulacrum of the rainbow bridge built by Wagner's all-too-human deities between earth and Walhalla. (Byatt, *Babel Tower*)

The point is that Schleiermacher's instinct for a universal hermeneutic was perfectly correct. Texts are sociable and relate to one another in a web of endless *intertextuality*. As readers we set up necessary distinctions between different genres and categories of texts like history, fiction, poetry, and philosophy, but, as we have seen, these are permeable in their claims to truth, and such terms as "history" as we understand it are modern inventions that would have been incomprehensible to the writers of the Gospels. Thus modern critics have begun to speak of them as "true fiction," presenting us as readers with a seeming paradox that our critical terminology has set up. (In the nineteenth century many people equated the term "fiction" simply with something that was "not true.")

Increasingly hermeneutics has come to acknowledge that we need to take intertextuality seriously, and this places a whole new light on the contemporary study of the Bible and the study of literature. When, in the seventeenth century, John Milton wrote his great "biblical" epic *Paradise Lost*, a fellow poet, Andrew Marvell, feared that it would be the "ruin of sacred truths," for such truths were absolute and the sole property of the Bible. But is this the case, and what is the status and claim of the poet who continues to explore in literature the great mysteries that are the biblical subjects? Is it the *truth* that is sacred or the *text*?

We now need to be very careful about what we mean by the word "text." Throughout this book we have assumed that it is a written body of words, even though the precise definition of that has varied between the Greek and the Hebrew traditions, and recent hermeneutics, like those of Stanley Fish, which have given more emphasis to the reader rather than to the text itself, have opened up ever-new questions about stability of meaning and reference. Still, it has remained a word-centered discussion, relating to books on our shelves and in our libraries. But increasingly we live within a culture that is *visual* as much (or perhaps more) than it is *verbal*, and we can now speak of "reading" the texts of film, or paintings and sculptures, and even the text of the body itself.

Thus, one of the recent developments in hermeneutical reflection on texts has been to extend our understanding of that word from the written word on the page to the "reading" of the visual image. Hermeneutics is no longer just about "the word" or words, but seeks to interpret varieties of "texts," perhaps in the Word made flesh. Actually this shift is not as new as it might seem. In the Middle Ages, Christ's body was frequently seen as a "text" to be read, his blood as it flowed down him from his wounds on the cross as a kind of ink, which inscribed the "words" of our salvation to be read as we contemplate the passion. A "hermeneutics of the body" is, in fact, ancient, as we think of the term as it was used by Paul in his letters, and this is now updated in the context of contemporary awareness of issues like gender, race, age, and so on. Furthermore if, reading the first chapter of the Fourth Gospel, we can speak of the Word made flesh, perhaps also we need to consider the hermeneutics of the flesh made word, a strategy with valuable *deconstructive* possibilities as we reflect on the stereotypes that we impress on the bodies of others in terms of their differences from us. People are defined by words like "masculine," "feminine," "mother," "black," and so on.

Increasingly I have found that the disciplinary barriers between literature and art are being broached, and nowhere more than in the study of the Bible. It has even been recently suggested that the painter Rembrandt is the greatest biblical critic ever to come out of the Netherlands. But how do we "read" a painting? Certainly it is not from beginning to end like a book—and so the principles of such reading must be quite different, and hermeneutics must adapt accordingly. Perhaps reading a painting or work of art is closer to what we have traditionally called *meditation*, but that suggestion is only just a start.

Furthermore, as we move ever farther into a predominately *visual* culture, in which films are often watched far more readily than books are read, hermeneutics is of necessity developing new skills in interpreting the *textuality of the screen*. Film is a textual medium distinct from the written narrative, with its own claims and its own authenticity. Let me give you just one simple example of why "reading" films as if they were just books (which is often the underlying assumption behind much of the current work on film and religion) is not hermeneutically good enough. The experience of seeing a film of a novel that we have read can often be odd, and frequently disappointing. The beautiful heroine who has bathed in the warm glow of our imagination as we read the book is simply not the actress who has been chosen to play the part on the screen, however beautiful she may be. In my experience she is just too much *there*, and has robbed my imagination of the luxury of seeing her in my mind from the few hints that the good novelist has given me. In short, watching a film can often be a disappointment to the imagination (which is a crucial element in our literary responses), and the harder the filmmaker tries by special effects or subtle lighting, the more disappointing it ultimately seems to be. But it is not that film cannot be enormously imaginative—it is just that you have to develop new interpretative skills of watching that are quite different from what goes on as you sit in your armchair with a good book. It is a different kind of text.

How should we, as students of "traditional" hermeneutics, respond to these developments in textuality, recognizing, perhaps, their ethical implications (as we see, for example, "body" as "text"). I referred earlier and briefly to the concept of *cyberspace*, and I cannot even begin to explore the hermeneutical implications of that here. What is interesting, however, is the way in which our computers mimic traditional textual forms as we write and read on them (my computer, for example, tells me that I am on page 87 of this text as I write these words!), but we cannot turn over the pages in the same way, or have a pile of different books open on our desks all at the same time for simultaneous reference. Reading and writing with computers is becoming a new art, and it will demand new hermeneutical insights.

Are our traditional skills, developed in all the ways we have seen, adequate for these new tasks, or will we have to develop new skills to meet new challenges? Schleiermacher, after all, saw hermeneutics as an art. As new art forms develop, do we have to discover hermeneutical arts to interpret them?

When the American abstract expressionist painter Jackson Pollock first showed his great "drip" paintings about fifty years ago, art critics were rendered speechless. They had no language to interpret such "texts." Now many would regard Pollock's works as deeply religious works of art—as religious texts. The feeling, experienced by many people, that these paintings are somehow "spiritual" is beginning to be translated into a critical language that gives expression to their mystery. It is a process that must happen to all great texts as we encounter them for the first time.

Summary

We might summarize the main points of this chapter as follows:

1. Hermeneutics is sensitive to cultural and technological change. Intepretation of texts, even ancient texts, can never stand still.
2. Reading modern literature that has been influenced by the Bible is important for our understanding of the Bible today.
3. Contemporary "liberation" hermeneutics allow for new ways of reading—and new responsibilities.
4. Hermeneutics must be sensitive to *political* shifts in a world that, for the West at least, is now very clearly "postcolonial."
5. The idea of the "text" is more than simply words written on a page; it extends to the "textuality" of pictures, movies, and even the human body itself. The extension of the idea of the text must also affect the concepts and practice of reading and interpretation.

Activities and Questions

1. The English poet William Blake (1757–1827) wrote in "A Memorable Fancy": "The prophets Isaiah and Ezekiel dined with me, and I asked them how they dared so roundly to assert that God spake to them; and whether they did not think at the time that they would be misunderstood, and so be the cause of imposition."

   Analyze this passage carefully. What does it suggest about poetic/divine inspiration? Is Blake, as a poet, claiming *equality* with the biblical prophets, and if so, is he justified in doing this? Why should the prophets fear misunderstanding? What do you think is meant here by the word "imposition"?

2. Here is an extract from J. Cheryl Exum's book *Plotted, Shot and Painted: Cultural Representations of Biblical Women.* It is taken from a chapter on the book of Hosea entitled "Prophetic Pornography," and refers to passages such as Hosea 2:9–10, in which the Lord threatens Israel for her "whore-

dom" in running after other gods, with nakedness to "uncover her shame in the sight of her lovers." Exum writes:

> I want to examine a particularly pernicious form of biblical violence against women where the perpetrator is not a collective, such as the army plundering cities, nor particular "evil men," but the deity himself: sexual violence where God appears as the subject and the object of his abuse is personified Israel/Judah/Jerusalem. The fact that this is metaphysical violence does not make it less criminal. (Exum, *Plotted, Shot and Painted*)

How do you respond to this? Does it make you go back to the biblical text of Hosea defensively, or with an intention to read it again, perhaps critically, in a new light? Do you find Professor Exum's words threatening or liberating? What do you think about the writer herself?

3. The Devil, who would lead us into the blindness of the heart and into the deafness of the mind, should be crucified, and care should be taken that his acolytes do not lift him down from the Cross to pursue the task of building Hell for the people on earth. (Ngũgĩ, *Devil on the Cross*)

Do you see any *implied* criticism of the passion narratives of the Gospels in this passage? Who do you think the Devil *is* here? How does this kind of literature (Ngũgî, remember, is a novelist) relate to the Bible?

4. Read this passage from the work of a modern scholar and biblical critic carefully, as a meditation on the body, and in particular the Christian concern with the body of Christ on the cross, as it lies at the very heart of Christianity as an *incarnational* (literally *embodied*) religion.

My own father too was a butcher, and a lover of lamb with mint sauce. As a child, the inner geographical boundaries of my world extended from the massive granite bulk of the Redemptorist church squatting at one end of our street to the butcher shop guarding the other end. Redemption, expiation, sacrifice, slaughter. . . . There was no city abbatoir in Limerick in those days; each butcher did his own slaughtering. I recall the hooks, the knives, the cleavers; the terror in the eyes of the victim; my own fear that I was afraid to show; the crude stun-gun slick with grease; the stunned victim collapsing to its knees; the slitting of the throat; the filling of the basins with blood; the skinning and evisceration of the carcass; the wooden barrels overflowing with entrails; the crimson floor littered with hooves. I also recall a Good Friday sermon by a Redemptorist preacher that recounted at remarkable length the atrocious agony felt by our sensitive Saviour as the spikes were driven through his wrists and feet. Crucifixion, crucifixation, crucasphyxiation. . . . Strange to say, it was this sombre recital, and not the other spectacle that finally caused me to faint. Helped outside by my father, I vomited gratefully on the steps of the church. (Stephen D. Moore, *God's Gym: Divine Male Bodies of the Bible*)

How do you respond to this passage? What is the writer saying? What does this say about certain Christian attitudes toward the human body?

5. Do you think that the figure of Jesus as portrayed in the Gospels makes a good movie role? There have been many "lives of Christ" on film, some of them profoundly religious, others scandalous or scurrilous. What relationship do they have to the texts of the four canonical Gospels?

Conclusion

The Sacred Text and the Future of Writing

Most of this book has been concerned with ways of reading the Bible. Jews and Christians, variously, read biblical texts and regard them as in some sense special, set apart or even "sacred." Some of the biblical stories are also to be found in the Qur'an, Islam being the other great "Abrahamic" religion. And there are many other sacred, or holy, texts in religious traditions, not to speak of those texts like the *Epic of Gilgamesh* which have survived from ancient cultures long after their religious traditions have perished and become lost in the mists of time.

Such books, in their various ways, have a remarkable capacity to survive and adapt. As we have seen with Luther and the invention of printing in Europe, they are often able to take advantage of technological developments successfully.

But our concern has not just been with such texts. Other textbooks have followed the history of biblical interpretation in detail, and our purpose has been rather different, though it has included some of that story. Rather, it has been with the activity of reading itself and how that has been perceived and engaged in across the millennia. We could have restricted ourselves to a concern with merely *literary hermeneutics*, but that would have been a narrower venture than the one we have been engaged in. The story of how texts like the epics of Homer, the great tragedies of Aeschylus and

Sophocles, or Virgil's *Aeneid*, Dante's *Divine Comedy*, or the plays of Shakespeare have been read and received in performance is by no means irrelevant to our concerns. Nor are the categories explored by modern literary theory such as formalism, reader-response criticism, structuralism, and semiotics. Actually many of these things we have discussed by implication, but it was not my purpose to get bogged down in technical terms, and there are plenty of good textbooks on literary theory if you want to go down that road. Werner Jeanrond has ascribed four aims to literary hermeneutics:

1. To examine a particular literary work or set of works
2. To examine the methods and effects of such interpretation
3. To study the structure of textual communication
4. To reflect upon the changing conditions of interpretation in our world (Jeanrond, *Theological Hermeneutics*)

But by focusing on the Bible as the text that has arguably driven more than any other the development of hermeneutics in Western culture, we have seen how our understanding of texts and the reading of *all literature* has an underlying theological concern. For almost all the hermeneuts we have studied have had a fundamental concern to ensure that we read the Word of God aright, and their practices have guided all our reading in one way or another. Hermeneutics is a thoroughly theological enterprise, and even though we may live in an age when theology is regarded very differently from the way in which Augustine, Aquinas, or Luther regarded it, the effects of what they did remain in all our reading as we continue to struggle with issues of the truth in writing, the inspiration of the text or its author, the origins of language, and so on.

But, as such phenomena as the World Wide Web become ever more available (though, like books in the Middle Ages, computers are still relatively the preserve of the educated and affluent), and the specter of cyberspace and information technology transforms our sense of *reality*, with its dimensions of time and space, into *hyperreality*, where no such dimensions exist, what is the future for the book, the written word, and the history of its interpretation? Overwhelmed by the information provided by information technology, we find it harder and harder to discriminate critically between one source and another. In other words, we need a new hermeneutics to recover our discrimination, for that is what hermeneutics sets out to do—give us guidance as we face choices in meaning or perhaps the option of believing in the truth of the four canonical Gospels of Matthew, Mark, Luke, and John rather than the claims of the many "apocryphal" Gospels of Thomas, Barnabas, Peter, and others.

It is probably too early to hazard an answer to all such questions. Already, back in the 1960s, postmodern critics like Derrida and Roland Barthes were contemplating the "end of the book," as its order falls apart in a maze of writing and words. And yet we are, in the great Abrahamic traditions at least, peoples of the Book and the sacred Word, and the word of the writer remains powerful and feared, and therefore to be understood. When the Russian Christian poet Irina Ratushinskaya was held in solitary confinement for her writing of verse (described as "anti-Soviet agitation and propaganda"), she continued to write, scratching out her poem "Pencil Letter" to her husband even though she never imagined that he or anyone else would ever read it.

> I know it won't be received
> Or sent. The page will be
> In shreds as soon as I have scribbled it.
> Later. Sometime. You've grown used to it,
> Reading between the lines that never reached you,
> Understanding everything.
> (Ratushinskaya, *Pencil Letter*)

Writing in prison, the poet has no reason to think that the fragile paper on which she is writing will survive to be read by the person for whom she is composing the poem. But texts are incredibly durable, and we now can read this poem, and we owe it to the poem and the spirit of the poet that we interpret it aright.

Hermeneutics today, as we saw in the last chapter, faces huge

challenges. But it remains as a fundamental activity in compre-
hension, an ethical demand on us that calls, as it has always done,
for all our resources of intellect and spirit. Some people have said
that, with its prophet Heidegger, postmodernity has brought about
the death of this great tradition whose history in the West we have
been following. It is, of course, only one tradition, and there are
others in other cultures which we have barely touched on.

What do you think of the future? Can we just retire to the study
with our books, announce business as usual, and hope that all this
nonsense with postmodernity and its aftermath, and all this new
technology, will go away? We have learned a great deal from those
who have gone before us, but does this mean that we have all the
answers? Or do we adapt our reading processes and continue to
interpret the Bible and other books in a new climate and a new
culture, with all its challenges?

What do you think?

Final Questions

1. Here are two interpretations of well-known biblical passages.
   The first is within the Bible itself, and is the interpretation of
   the parable of the sower in Mark 4:14–20, placed in the
   mouth of Jesus himself:

   > The sower sows the word. These are the ones on the path
   > where the word is sown: when they hear, Satan immedi-
   > ately comes and takes away the word that is sown in them.
   > And these are the ones sown on rocky ground: when they
   > hear the word, they immediately receive it with joy. But
   > they have no root, and endure only for a while; then, when
   > trouble or persecution arises on account of the word,
   > immediately they fall away. And others are those sown
   > among the thorns: these are the ones who hear the word,
   > but the cares of the world, and the lure of wealth, and the
   > desire for other things come in and choke the word, and it
   > yields nothing. And these are the ones sown on the good
   > soil: they hear the word and accept it and bear fruit, thirty
   > and sixty and a hundredfold.

The second is Augustine's interpretation of the parable of the good Samaritan from Luke's Gospel, to be found in his *Quaestiones Evangeliorum*, II, 19:

> *A certain man went down from Jerusalem to Jericho*; Adam himself is meant; *Jerusalem* is the heavenly city of peace, from whose blessedness Adam fell; *Jericho* means the moon, and signifies our mortality, because it is born, waxes, wanes, and dies. *Thieves* are the devil, and his angels. *Who stripped him*, namely, of his immortality; *and beat him*, by persuading him to sin; *and left him half-dead*, because in so far as man can understand and know God, he lives, but in so far as he is wasted and oppressed by sin, he is dead; he is therefore called *half-dead*. The *priest* and *Levite* who saw him and passed by, signify the priesthood and ministry of the Old Testament, which could profit nothing for salvation. *Samaritan* means Guardian, and therefore the Lord Himself is signified by this name. *The binding of the wounds* is the restraint of sin. *Oil* is the comfort of good hope; *wine* is the exhortation to work with fervent spirit. The *beast* is the flesh in which He deigned to come to us. The being *set upon the beast* is the belief in the incarnation of Christ. The *inn* is the Church, where travellers returning to their heavenly country are refreshed after pilgrimage. The *morrow* is after the resurrection of the Lord. The *two pence* are either the two precepts of love, or the promise of this life and of that which is to come. The *innkeeper* is the Apostle (Paul). The supererogatory payment is either his counsel of celibacy, or the fact that he worked with his own hands lest he should be a burden to any of the weaker brethren when the Gospel was new, though it was lawful for him "to live by the Gospel." (Quoted in C. H. Dodd, *The Parables of the Kingdom*)

What are the strengths and weaknesses of these two allegorical readings?

2. In what ways has a knowledge of hermeneutics made you a better reader? Has it enabled you to understand the Bible more clearly?

Bibliography

Abrams, M. H. *Natural Supernaturalism: Tradition and Revolution in Romantic Literature.* New York: W. W. Norton & Co., 1971.

Aristotle. *On the Art of Poetry.* Translated by T. S. Dorsch. In *Aristotle, Horace, Longinus: Classical Literary Criticism.* Harmondsworth, Middlesex: Penguin, 1965.

Atwood, Margaret. *The Handmaid's Tale.* 1985. London: Vintage, 1996.

Augustine, *City of God.* Translated by Henry Bettenson. Harmondsworth, Middlesex: Penguin, 1972.

———. *Confessions.* Translated by R. S. Pine-Coffin. Harmondsworth, Middlesex: Penguin, 1961.

Barth, Karl. *The Epistle to the Romans.* Translated from the 6th ed. by Edwyn C. Hoskyns. 1933. Oxford: Oxford University Press, 1968.

Beckerlegge, Gwilym, ed. *The World Religions Reader.* London and New York: Routledge, 1998.

Blake, William. "A Memorable Fancy." 1790. Reprinted in John Drury, ed., *Critics of the Bible, 1724–1873.* Cambridge: Cambridge University Press, 1989.

Bruns, Gerald L. *Hermeneutics Ancient and Modern.* New Haven, Conn., and London: Yale University Press, 1992.

Byatt, A. S. *Babel Tower.* London: Vintage, 1997.

Carroll, Lewis. *Alice's Adventures in Wonderland* (1965); *Through the Looking Glass* (1971). In *The Annotated Alice,* edited by Martin Gardner. Harmondsworth, Middlesex: Penguin, 1970.

Chladenius, Johann Martin. *Introduction to the Correct Interpretation of Reasonable Discourses and Writings.* 1742. In *The Hermeneutics Reader,* edited by Kurt Mueller-Vollmer. Oxford: Blackwell, 1986.

Coleridge, Samuel Taylor. *Confessions of an Inquiring Spirit.* 3d ed. 1853. Philadelphia: Fortress Press, 1988.

Cross, F. L., and E. A. Livingstone, eds. *The Oxford Dictionary of the Christian Church.* 3d ed. Oxford: Oxford University Press, 1997.

Culler, Jonathan. *Saussure.* London: Fontana, 1976.

Derrida, Jacques. *Of Grammatology.* Translated by Gayatri Chakravorty Spivak. Baltimore and London: Johns Hopkins University Press, 1976.

Dodd, C. H. *The Parables of the Kingdom.* Rev. ed. London: James Nisbet, 1961.

Eckhart, Meister. *Selected Writings.* Translated by Oliver Davies. Harmondsworth, Middlesex: Penguin, 1994.

Eliot, T. S. *Selected Essays.* 3d ed. London: Faber and Faber, 1951.

Elwood, Christopher. *Calvin for Armchair Theologians.* Louisville, Ky.: Westminster John Knox Press, 2002.

Erasmus, Desiderius. *The Essential Erasmus.* Translated by John P. Dolan. London: New English Library, 1964.

Exum, J. Cheryl. *Plotted, Shot and Painted: Cultural Representations of Biblical Women.* Sheffield: Sheffield Academic Press, 1996.

Fish, Stanley. *Is There a Text in This Class? The Authority of Interpretive Communities.* Cambridge, Mass: Harvard University Press, 1980.

Frei, Hans W. *The Eclipse of Biblical Narrative: A Study in Eighteenth and Nineteenth Century Hermeneutics.* New Haven, Conn., and London: Yale University Press, 1974.

Gosse, Edmund. *Father and Son: A Study of Two Temperaments.* 1907. Harmondsworth, Middlesex: Penguin, 1976.

Grant, Robert M. with David Tracy. *A Short History of the Interpretation of the Bible.* Philadelphia: Fortress Press, 1984.

Habermas, Jürgen. *The Philosophical Discourse of Modernity.* Translated by Frederick Lawrence. Cambridge: Polity Press, 1987.

Handelman, Susan A. *The Slayers of Moses: The Emergence of Rabbinic Interpretation in Modern Literary Theory.* Albany: State University of New York Press, 1982.

Hartman, Geoffrey H. "The Struggle for the Text." In *Midrash and Literature*, edited by Geoffrey H. Hartman and Sanford Budick. New Haven, Conn., and London: Yale University Press, 1986.

Jeanrond, Werner G. *Theological Hermeneutics: Development and Significance.* London: Macmillan, 1991.

Jobling, David, Tina Pippin, and Ronald Schleifer, eds. *The Postmodern Bible Reader.* Oxford: Basil Blackwell, 2001.

Kant, Immanuel. "An Answer to the Question: 'What Is Enlightenment?'" 1784. In *Political Writings*, 2d ed., edited by Hans Reiss. Cambridge: Cambridge University Press, 1991.

Klemm, David E. *Hermeneutical Inquiry.* Two volumes. American Academy of Religion Studies in Religion, 43, 44. Atlanta: Scholars Press, 1986.

Kocklemans, Joseph J. *On the Truth of Being: Reflections on Heidegger's Later Philosophy.* Bloomington: Indiana University Press, 1984.

LaCocque, André and Paul Ricoeur. *Thinking Biblically: Exegetical and Hermeneutical Studies.* Translated by David Pellauer. Chicago and London: University of Chicago Press, 1998.

Lowth, Robert, *Lectures on the Sacred Poetry of the Hebrews*. 1753. English translation by Richard Gregory, 1787. Extracts in *Critics of the Bible, 1724–1873*, edited by John Drury. Cambridge: Cambridge University Press, 1989.

Luther, Martin. *Table Talk*. Translated by William Hazlitt. London: Fount Paperbacks, 1995.

Moore, Stephen D. *God's Gym: Divine Male Bodies of the Bible*. New York and London: Routledge, 1996.

Moule, C. F. D. *The Birth of the New Testament*. 2d ed. London: Adam & Charles Black, 1966.

Neusner, Jacob. *What Is Midrash?* Philadelphia: Fortress Press, 1987.

Ngũgĩ wa Thiong'o. *Devil on the Cross*. 1982. London: Heinemann, 1987.

Page, Nick. *The Tabloid Bible*. Louisville, Ky.: Westminster John Knox Press, 1998.

Plato. *The Phaedrus* and Letters VII and VIII. Translated by Walter Hamilton. Harmondsworth, Middlesex: Penguin, 1973.

Ratushinskaya, Irina. *Pencil Letter*. Newcastle-upon-Tyne: Bloodaxe Books, 1988.

Ricoeur, Paul. *Figuring the Sacred: Religion, Narrative and Imagination*. Translated by David Pellauer. Minneapolis: Fortress Press, 1995.

———. *Oneself as Another*. Translated by Kathleen Blamey. Chicago and London: University of Chicago Press, 1992.

———. *The Symbolism of Evil*. Translated by Emerson Buchanan. Boston: Beacon Press, 1969.

Schweitzer, Albert. *The Quest of the Historical Jesus*. 1906. Edited and translated by John Bowden. London: SCM Press, 2000.

Stevenson, J., ed. *A New Eusebius: Documents Illustrative of the History of the Church to A.D. 337*. London: S.P.C.K., 1960.

Sugirtharajah, R. S. *Postcolonial Criticism and Biblical Interpretation*. Oxford: Oxford University Press, 2002.

Thomas à Kempis. *The Imitation of Christ*. Translated by Leo Sherley-Price. Harmondsworth, Middlesex: Penguin, 1952.

Index of Names and Titles of Works

Numbers in bold indicate main discussions.

Index of Subjects

Numbers in bold indicate main discussions.